THE CULTURAL HISTORY OF
RUSSIA

THE CULTURAL HISTORY OF
RUSSIA

TEXT BY ASTRID BORG

Cover

The Cathedral of St. Basil at Moscow, built under the reign of Ivan the Terrible (sixteenth century), is a very representative specimen of Russian architecture.

Endpapers

"The Fighting Church", seventeenth century icon.

Title page

The Cathedral of the Annunciation at the Kremlin in Moscow was built in the years 1484-1489 by architects from Pskov. It associates the characteristics of Pskovian and Muscovite architecture and it was used as a private chapel by the Tsars.

ISBN 0-906053-68-4

Contents

The Birth of a Nation

Russia was for a long time a country about which very little was known, and for many people it still is. For those who do set out to discover it, the universe which reveals itself often appears too broad to comprehend: it is fascinating in its extremes, and rich in contrasts and diverse influences. The sheer immensity of the territories which combine to make Russia give it this multifarious character. Some people see Russia as a bridge joining Europe and Asia; others go to great lengths to emphasize either the occidental or the oriental side of its cultural and artistic expression. But against these arguments must be weighed the uniformity of the terrain, which has left its stamp on Russian art and, more important, has determined certain characteristic features of its architecture.

An immense land

Russian nationalist historians trace the birth of Russia back to Scythian times (7th to 1st centuries B.C.), considering the Scythians as the ancestors of the Slavs. But according to the version more generally favoured by historians, it dates from the Christian conversion brought about under Byzantine influence in 988 A.D.; and up until the 20th century the borders of Russia have continued to change a great deal. The Scythians principally occupied the territories of southern Russia, while the great empire which had Kiev as its capital was confined to the Dnieper valley. But the campaigns mounted by the tsars, with Moscow as their base, following their deliverance from the domination of the Mongols, were to push the frontiers of Russia out as far as the Pacific. Siberia was thus incorporated into Russian territory in the 17th century. Renewed territorial expansion under Peter the Great further integrated great tracts of the Baltic countries—Estonia, Latvia and Karelia, as well as the western coastline of the Caspian Sea—into Russia. Ultimately the influence of Russia was to extend to the Caucasus and central Asia. In the middle of the 19th century, Russian possessions spanned three continents: Europe, Asia, and—until the cession of Alaska in 1867—North America.

Territorial variety and diversity of peoples, cultures and influences—herein lies one of the essential characteristics of the Russian world and its art. These influences are numerous as well as varied. It is sometimes argued that there is no such thing as Russian art, strictly speaking, and that Russian artistic expression is nothing more than a patchwork of foreign elements, of either eastern or western origin.

This diversity, due as it was to the geographical location of Russia and to the mercantile contacts which followed from this, was compounded by Peter the Great when he opened Russia to the West. The imprint of French, Italian and German art can be identified in Russian art of the period. Russian art was, however, enriched by these foreign elements rather than impoverished by them, and was able to retain its originality.

There is a certain Russian means of artistic expression, the originality of which is closely linked to the Russian way of life, which itself is determined by specific climatic conditions and by a particular natural environment. The harshness of the winters, during which temperatures may fall as low as −50°C (−60°F), alternate with often torrid summers; autumn and spring are merely brief periods in which the ground becomes waterlogged by the rains or melting snow, cutting off villages

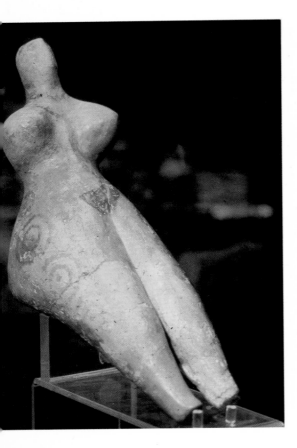

Scythian statuette; 4th millenium B.C. (Hermitage Museum, Leningrad).

lost in the vast Russian plain. It is in the course of these winters, which in some areas may last for up to seven or eight months, that the Russian peasant (the majority of the Russian population inhabits rural areas), thrown back on his own resources, spends his days creating the essential articles of everyday life—distaffs for spinning, porringers, and so on. By virtue of the excellence of the workmanship, these have often come to be regarded as works of art.

Elsewhere Russian artists and, even more important, the architects were to take the forms inherited from Byzantium and adapt them to their

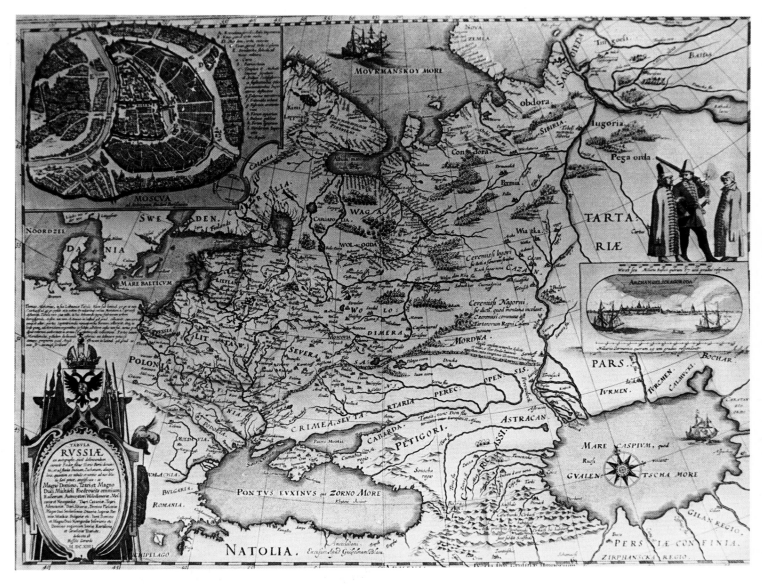

own rude climate, eventually leading to the familiar and specifically Russian forms in which wood is the building material. To this end the openings giving access to the buildings, particularly churches, became narrower; the roofs were pitched at an angle to prevent the accumulation of water and snow: the architects endeavoured to integrate their buildings in a harmonious union with the Russian landscape, the dominant feature of which is the immense plain that stretches from the western frontiers to the Yenisei, only briefly interrupted by the Urals. Then there are the plateaux and mountains of eastern Siberia, and, in the south, the Caucasian mountain chain (reaching a height of 5633 metres—18,480 feet) and that of Pamir (highest point 7495 metres—24,591 feet). It is, however, the infinite plain that remains the dominant feature of this landscape. Its vegetation and its forests provided wood, the material commonly used to fashion the objects necessary to daily life, and to construct the *isbas* (dwellings), the towns, the earliest *kremlins* (fortified towns) and the churches, as well as to make those masterpieces of Russian painting, the icons.

The Scythians settled from the 6th century B.C. in southern Russia, in the hinterland of the Black Sea.

Following pages:
The vase of Chertomlyk, 6th-4th centuries B.C.: one of the finest works of Scythian art, in which the influence of Greece is predominant (Hermitage Museum, Leningrad).

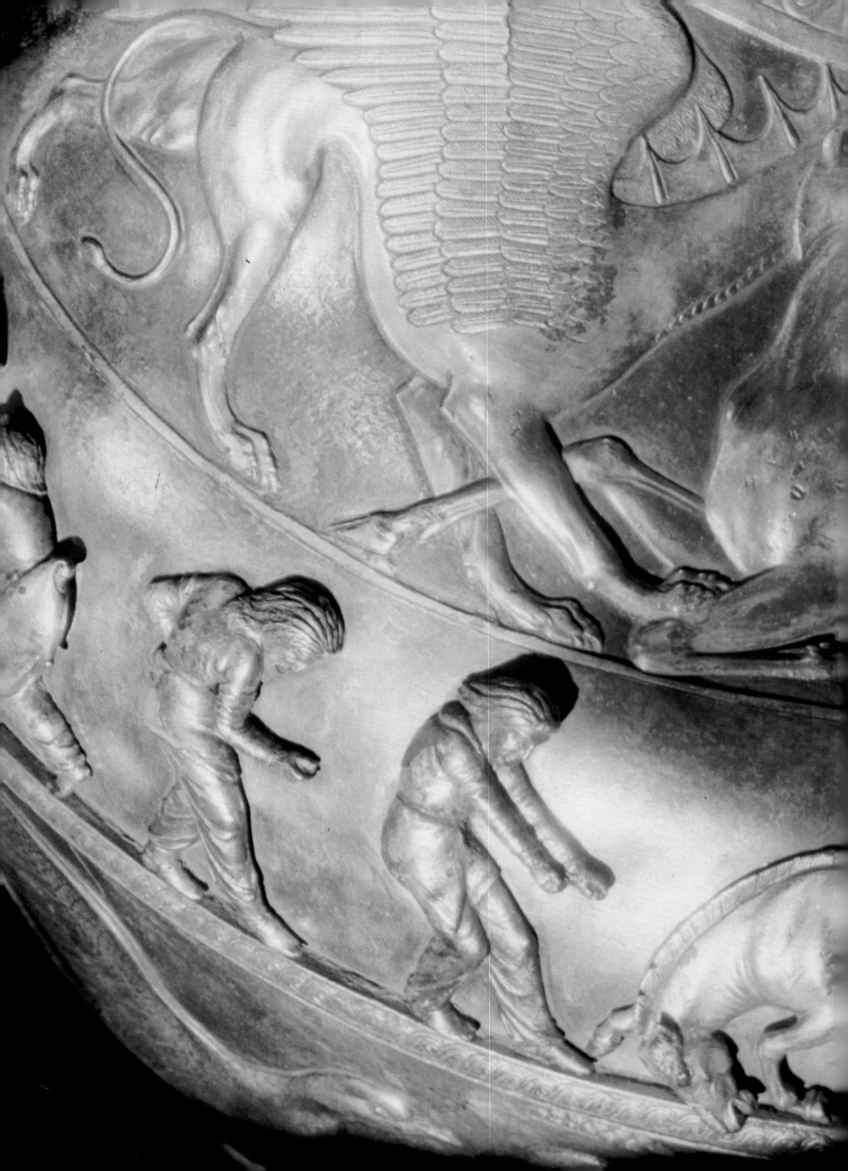

This is the territory, exceptional in various respects, upon which the Russian race was born. In the 18th century and subsequently the Russians have attempted to trace their origins back to the Scythians—a people whose own origins and lives were for a long time surrounded by legends set down by Herodotus. More recently the role they played in the formation of the Russian people has been understood with a greater degree of insight.

The Scythians

Originally from Asia, the Scythians had already conquered numerous lands—including Medicia, Palestine and Syria—and subsequently lost them again, when in the 6th century they finally settled in southern Russia, occupying the hinterland of the Black Sea. This territory was divided

Above and right:
Horse and funeral carriage, 5th century
B.C. (Hermitage Museum, Leningrad).

into four regions, each of which was administrated by a governor, whose duty it was to collect the tributes. These regions correspond to four recognized groups: royal Scythians, agricultural Scythians, labouring Scythians and nomadic Scythians, whose responsibilities varied as their titles suggest. The royal Scythians, whose social structure had evolved from a matriarchy into a patriarchy, were the ones to govern the confederation and to appoint the governors of the regions. The Scythians maintained excellent relations with the Greeks, to whom they supplied wheat, wood, cattle and honey, and with whom they shared the profits from the numerous Greek finance-houses established on the banks of the Black Sea.

Each of the groups had its own characteristic life-style. This was highly adventurous in the case of the nomadic Scythians, who were responsible for the safety of the herds; the horse played a vital role in their lives and is very widely represented in their art. The life of the settled Scythians who applied themselves to fishing and agriculture was more peaceful. But all of them were united by strict observance of

Bronze mask; 6th–4th century B.C. (Hermitage Museum, Leningrad).

customs, and by a religion the distinguishing features of which were the importance of sorcery, of worship of the great goddess, and of gory funeral rites. When a king died large numbers of prisoners were put to death, along with his most faithful servants, his concubines and countless horses. The victims of these mass sacrifices were buried together with the king and huge numbers of articles of value, all accompanying him on his last voyage in the tomb. The tombs lay beneath the tumuli or *kurgans* which are to be found over extensive tracts of Russian territory; and archaeologists have discovered inside them the finest examples of Scythian art. It is regrettable that a certain number of them had been ransacked or investigated by amateurs before 1859, when the Imperial Archaeological Commission was given the task of supervising and directing the explorations in an orderly scientific fashion.

Animals in one form or another feature in the majority of Scythian works of art. Often they—or parts of their bodies—are represented in a form so stylized that they are scarcely distinguishable from the purely decorative figures that adorn the object in question.

11

However, the Scythians were not content merely to manufacture weapons and decorate them, using metal as their raw material. They also delighted in the use of gold to create objects of rare beauty such as the golden comb of Solokha (4th century B.C.), or jewellery such as the set belonging to the queen buried at Kul Oba, which consists of a diadem, a necklace of lions' heads, and bracelets ornamented with gryphons devouring deer. The craft of these goldsmiths, very much influenced by Greek art, can be clearly distinguished from Perso-Scythian art by its marked oriental character: inlaid glass, coloured or precious stones, and a more crude stylization (e.g. the treasure of Novocherkassk). Taking these diverse influences and characteristics into account, Scythian art objects are subdivided into four groups as follows:

Dnieper group—the most valuable objects that belong to this, the westernmost group are the silver vase of Chertomlyk and the solid gold comb of Solokha.

Kerch group (Crimea)—distinguished by the jewellery discovered in the tumulus of Kul Oba and by the diadem from the tumulus of Artiukha.

Don and Kuban group—the jewellery from the tumulus of Karagodenashkh and the *kurgan* of Ulski, where four hundred horses were buried complete with harness, are of particular interest in this group.

Siberian and Central Asian group—the easternmost of the Scythian treasures is that of the Amu Darya, where coins from the 2nd and 1st centuries B.C. were found together with golden plates.

In the more recent past efforts have been made to unearth the ruins of Scythian towns, especially Neapolis which was capital of the Crimea in the 4th century B.C. These explorations are helping to build up our picture—a picture which is still hazy and incomplete in places—of a race of people and an art that have a number of highly intriguing facets.

The ancient Slavs

The origin of the word "Slav" is disputed. However, it seems likely that it is derived from "slovo", which means "word" in Russian and hence is used to designate all those who can communicate with the same words. The word Slav itself is generic and designates a group of tribes, among them the "Rus"—a term which was eventually extended to cover all of the Slavs from the east. The Slavs first made their appearance on present-day Russian soil in the 6th century A.D., and settled in the area between the Vistula, the Dnieper and the Carpathian mountains. It is no coincidence that the main communications route between the north (Scandinavia and the Baltic) and the south (Byzantium and the Black Sea) follows the course of the Dnieper. This route was a formative influence on the evolution of the Russian economy and civilization, for upon it the most important centres of ancient Russia grew up: Kiev, Chernigov, Smolensk and Novgorod. Furthermore, it was the necessity of defending this commercial lifeline and its developing towns against the incessant aggression of the nomadic tribes, that induced the Slavs to call on the Varangians, or Norsemen, for assistance at the beginning of the 9th century: they themselves were too disorganized and divided, and thus too weak, to defend their own lands.

There is, unfortunately, little evidence relating to the life and culture of the ancient Slavs; the seven centuries separating the Scythians from the Christian conversion of Russia are to a large extent hidden under a veil of darkness. There are two reasons for the dearth of monuments and works of art dating from this period. The first is that wood was used almost exclusively in the construction of both temples and villages—and wood is a material that does not easily withstand the ravages of time; the second is the spread of the Christian faith, the converted princes ordering the destruction of everything connected with pagan customs and

Stylized statuettes; "The Warrior's Rest" (4th century B.C.) and "Battle Scene" (Hermitage Museum, Leningrad).

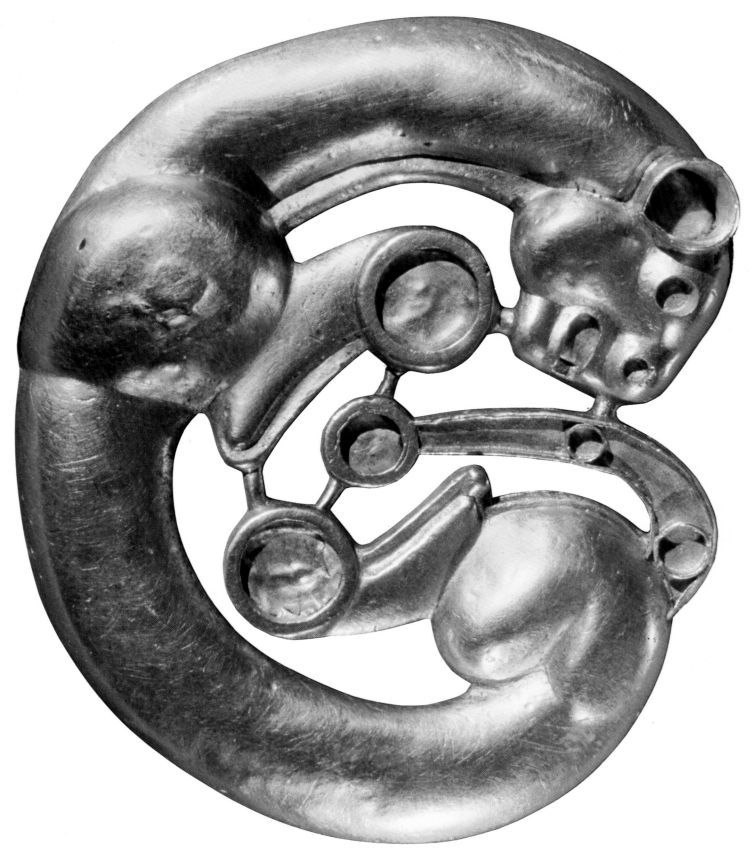

practices. Thus literature is the only real source of information which permits us to provide a rough sketch of the life of the people during this period. They lived in villages of wooden or cob-walled houses, surrounded with palisades and built for the most part on the precipitous banks of lakes and rivers.

The ancient Slavs were pagans, and they worshipped their numerous deities in elaborately carved wooden temples, as well as in the open air in the clearings of sacred forests. The chief god of the northern Slavs, a creature with four heads and four necks named Svantovit, had an annual festival held in his honour—a tradition which continued long after the conversion of the Russians to Christianity. On these occasions, the high

Stylized lion (Hermitage Museum, Leningrad).

13

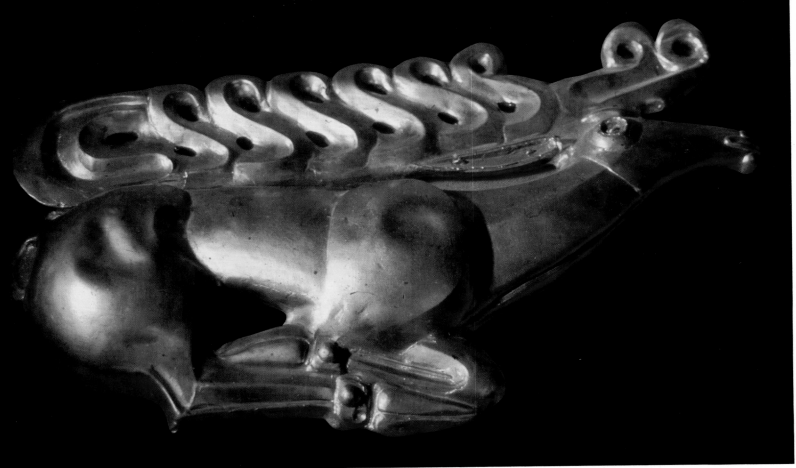

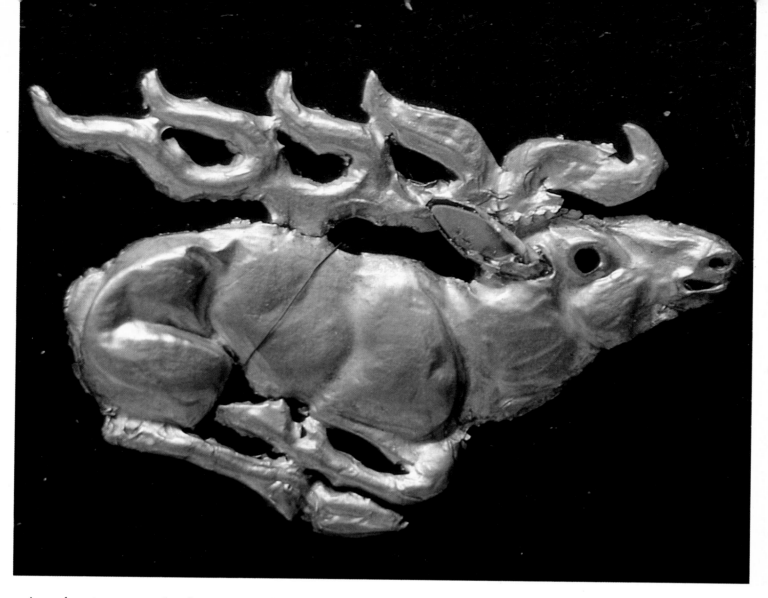

priest alone was permitted to approach the statue of the god and fill his horn (one of the attributes of the godhead) with spirituous liquor. For the southern Slavs it is Perun, the god of thunder, who seems to have held supremacy over the others. In his honour a fire was kept burning night and day near his statue. Around him are Volos, god of the sun, and Mokos, goddess of the rain and of the earth and doubtless the successor of the great goddess of the Scythians. There were also many other divinities, worshipped in more or less brilliant and gory ceremonies. These gods were assisted in day-to-day routine by a host of goblins and other spirits that peopled nature and frequented dwelling-places, e.g. the genie of the house (domostrozh), the spirit of water (vodianozh), and others. Almost all the material evidence of this entire period had soon disappeared. Despite this the memory of all these gods and spirits lived on for a long time, rooted in the Slav consciousness, running parallel to the Christian faith and insinuating itself into it.

Thus until the 10th century Slav society was a tribal one, the number of the tribes being equalled only by the number of gods they worshipped. In the absence of a powerful and structured body politic the tribes could rely on certain freedoms, but the inevitable consequence was a lack of unity which rendered them vulnerable to pressure from outside. For the first time in the history of the Slavs, the introduction of the Christian faith put an end to this disorganized structure; in this sense the consequences went beyond the purely spiritual plane.

The Christian conversion

The trading links between the Slavs and Byzantium had been strong for a very long time: the Slavs came to sell off their wares, such as honey and furs, on the steps of the "Imperial city" (*Tsargorod* in Russian). This

Deer (Hermitage Museum, Leningrad). Animal art is highly stylized, and is concerned with the depiction of both real and fabulous animals.

Opposite page:
Mounted horseman from Kul Oba, 4th century B.C. (Hermitage Museum, Leningrad.)

Golden moose; probably 5th century B.C. (Hermitage Museum, Leningrad.)

Below:
*Scythian bracelet. Scythian objects of art
demonstrate the twofold influences of
Greece and the Orient: in this case Greek
influence with its fine engraving prevails
(Hermitage Museum, Leningrad).*

Above:
*Oriental influence can be seen in a
preference for the inlaying of precious
stones, often on objects that are less finely
engraved.*

Opposite page:
*Golden Scythian comb from Solokha, 4th
century B.C. (Hermitage Museum,
Leningrad).*

relationship was not always entirely without an aggressive element; the
wealth of Byzantium aroused the covetous instincts of the Russian rulers,
just as it did for many others. However the Russians never succeeded in
conquering the pearl of the Orient, while for its part Byzantium had a
significant influence on Russia, and considerably before the baptism of
Vladimir in 988 there had been a number of Slav converts. Nevertheless
it was the conversion of the Grand Prince Vladimir that marked a turn-
ing point in the history of Russia: the introduction of Christianity as the
official religion had consequences of major importance on the political,
cultural and artistic level.

Vladimir left Byzantium accompanied by Greek priests whose mission
was to convert and baptise his people, and this they carried out on a
massive scale in the waters of the Dnieper. What was not so easy was to
abolish at one stroke the secular beliefs which hitherto had dominated
the lives of these people, and inevitably certain pagan customs and
beliefs survived in Russia well beyond the 10th century.

This Christian conversion was also closely bound up with the establishment of a political structure which, after the example of the religious hierarchy, was centralized. Thus, for the first time a unity of sorts was created among the Russian people, based on submission to the power of the grand prince of Kiev. It was also at this time that the Cyrillic alphabet was introduced in Russia: based on the Greek alphabet, it was propagated by means of the holy books that were translated into old Slavonic by Cyril and Methodius, the bishops of Salonica. The Slavs in the west—the Poles and Czechs—opted instead for the Latin alphabet and Latin religious rites, and this opened a deep rift between the Slavs of the west and those of the east. The Slavs of the east, however, cut off though they were from Rome on the religious level, maintained good economic and diplomatic relations with the west.

There is no question that it is in the realm of art that the influence of

Byzantium on Russia was most deeply felt. The early impetus came from Byzantium, even though the Russians adapted the Byzantine models to a Russian context and gave them their own original stamp. The characteristic features of the churches of Byzantium can be identified in the churches of Kiev and Novgorod: Russian artists and architects drew inspiration from the churches of Santa Sophia and of the Holy Apostles (a church with five cupolas) or again, from the layout and decoration of the New Church of Byzantium.

The princely town of Kiev

So, for the first time, the Russians were to live in a State, with Kiev as its capital. This State nevertheless retained the characteristics of a family estate, the inheritance—and thus the land—being divided up between the sons of the grand prince on his death. The resultant internal quarelling was more injurious to Kievan Russia than all the threats from outside: fratricidal struggles eventually brought about the downfall of Kiev, mother of Russian towns, the beauty and wealth of which had dazzled no small number of foreign travellers.

Three grand princes, Vladimir, Yaroslav and Iziaslav are the key figures in the artistic and cultural history of Kievan Russia. They made use of the resources drawn from agriculture and their flourishing commerce (the amber route passed through Kievan Russia) to bewstow upon

Opposite page, top and centre:
*"Wild-boar Hunt": rock-paintings found
in the ancient Scythian town of Neapolis,
dating from the 3rd–1st centuries B.C.*

Left:
*Icon depicting Cyril and Methodius, the
bishops of Salonica.*

Opposite page, bottom:
*An antique Slav god (Museum of
Archaeology, Copenhagen).*

the town its most beautiful monuments: the Church of the Dormition, the Cathedral of Santa Sophia, the monastery of catacombs, St. Michael with the Gold Cupolas, and St. Cyril of Alexandria. At the beginning of the 11th century there were no less than 400 churches in Kiev, not to mention the numerous civil buildings, which included palaces and the wealthy houses of the boyars who administrated the lands of the princes.

There is relatively little left standing from this glorious age, numerous monuments and churches having been pillaged by the nomadic (and sometimes native Russian) plunderers, then destroyed once and for all in the Mongol invasion. Among others the Church of the Dormition of the Virgin was lost in this way.

However, that which has come down to us despite the ravages of time is evidence of remarkable architectural and artistic activity. One such building is the Cathedral of Santa Sophia, constructed in 1037, in which, although damaged and not altogether successfully restored in the 17th and 18th centuries, former splendours may still be seen.

Perhaps the most striking thing of all is the beauty of the mosaics. The subjects depicted in these are very varied: St. Mark the Evangelist, Christ preaching, St. John the Baptist, the Archangel Gabriel, and above all the Eucharist, with the apostles above whom Christ is enthroned (some observers see a parallel between this image and the grand prince ruling over his subjects). The expressive quality of the faces and the lifelike animation of their features engage our attention, while the persons in

19

the mosaic entitled *The celestial order* seem stiffer and more severe. But the best-known of the mosaics, and the one most surrounded by legend, is that of the Virgin Orans; this is imposing enough for its size alone. With her long robe draped about her, hands raised in a gesture of prayer, she reigns together with the Almighty in the cupola and intercedes with him on behalf of men. According to popular legend it was she who protected the wall which her image adorns from destruction when the entire edifice of the Church of Santa Sophia collapsed during construction; this wall became generally known as "the indestructible wall" as a consequence. The art of the mosaic was more widely practised and appreciated in Kiev than anywhere else. The mosaics of Kiev were typical of this essentially Byzantine art form, particularly favoured for the decoration of churches, and were executed either by craftsmen from Byzantium or by Russian artists who had taken the decorations of Byzantine churches as their model. In no other Russian artistic centre are they to be found in such numbers: in Novgorod, Suzdal and Moscow frescoes are preferred, along with the more authentically Russian icons. Nevertheless, mural-painting was already becoming well established in Kievan Russia. In the Church of Santa Sophia it attracts the visitor's attention by both the quality of the workmanship and the nature of the subjects chosen—traditional religious subjects can be found side by side with secular ones. In the north tower of the church there is a bear-hunting

"The Fathers of the Church", mosaic. Cathedral of Santa Sophia of Kiev.

The Cathedral of Santa Sophia of Kiev (left) was built in 1037 at the highest point of the town, and in spite of the restoration work carried out in the 17th and 18th centuries it remains one of the most remarkable monuments of ancient Russia to have survived to the present day.

Opposite page, bottom:
"Virgin of Novgorod", Cathedral of Santa Sophia.

scene, while in the south tower a depiction of strolling musicians and players is on view. Animals, both imaginary (gryphons) and real (a panther and a camel with camel-driver) are also present. One of the walls is taken up with the grand prince and the kniazin Irina with her three daughters holding candles in their hands. These profane images are, however, confined to the towers housing the stairways that lead directly from the galleries of the church to the adjoining palace. Within the sacred walls of the church itself there is a preponderance of religious subjects: St. Maxime and the Archangel Michael, St. Nicholas and the Archdeacon Lavrenti, the Annunciation—all frescoes dating from the 11th century. They are remarkable for the perfection of the workmanship and the fine proportions of the faces. This artistic mastery is also evident in the decoration of the tombs of princes buried in the church, such as the tomb of Yaroslav.

There is only one fresco in Kievan Russia that antedates those in the Church of Santa Sophia—that of St. Fekla in the Church of the Transfiguration in Chernigov; this dates from around 1030–1040 whereas the frescoes of Santa Sophia were created towards the end of the 11th century. (This cathedral was plundered by the Tartars in 1240, and subsequently by the Poles also.) The fresco of St. Fekla stands out by virtue of the subtle tones of the colours used, which give to the saint's face an expression of benevolence and great gentleness, and which affirm that this is the work of an accomplished master. The cathedral was constructed in 1031 by Greek builders from Constantinople on the orders of Vladimir's son. As in other religious buildings the cupola is the principal element in terms of both construction and decoration, and in its conception it is exactly like those of Constantinople. Even so, there are certain elements of the cathedral which seem to have been borrowed from Roman art, and some have detected in it the influence of Armenian architecture of the Caucasus, which reached its apogee in the 10th and 11th centuries.

The mosaics of the Monastery of St. Michael, which dates from the

end of the 10th century, constitute another masterpiece of Byzantine art; they stand out on account of the skill with which the figures have been formed, and the richness of their coloration. In the opinion of the archdeacon Pavel Alepiski, who visited Kiev in 1653 and 1655, these mosaics are surprisingly reminiscent of those at Santa Sophia in the choice of subjects for treatment: the Virgin Orans is to be found once again here, as is the Eucharist group dominating the frieze of Saints. The Almighty reigns over the cupola in the traditional fashion. However, the execution of the mosaics of St. Michael differs markedly from that of Santa Sophia, in terms of both form and composition. At Santa Sophia the apostles are depicted in an attitude that is uniform and stylized, rigid and severe; at St. Michael they represent a radically different approach to composition, and they convey a sense of movement. Here they are not standing uniformly spaced, but mingle in small groups, although still surrounding Christ in order to share with him the secret of communion. Each individual apostle is given a different expression and has different facial features, conveying welcome in this case, surprise in the other; there is, in fact, a psychological dimension which confers a special place on the apostles of St. Michael in Russian art. Apart from this, in the portrayal of the faces the eyes are not emphasized at the expense of the other features (wide-open eyes which seem to gaze upon eternity are a distinguishing characteristic of Byzantine painting); the artist has taken pains to achieve the correct proportions in the features, so as not to give special treatment to one part of the face to the detriment of the rest.

Religious art is pre-eminent during this period, but secular art is not without its works of beauty. The treasure of Tversk comprises some superb jewels, including a pair of star-shaped silver earrings dating from the 11th or 12th century. The golden diadem of Sakhonovka also dates from the 11th century. At the same time the art of illumination, the finest examples of which are currently kept in the Saltikov-Shchedrin Library, was becoming more and more widespread.

However, in spite of—or perhaps because of—its glorious ascendancy, Kievan Russia had not the power to resist the threats and pressures to which it was subjected. In 1109 Kiev was sacked, and this fatal blow initiated its downfall. It was a Russian prince, Andrei Bogoliubski, who organized the sacking of Kiev and the transfer of the capital to Vladimir. The great cultural tradition was all that remained, and this was continued in Smolensk and Novgorod, in Vladimir-Suzdal and in Riazan, where it came to magnificent fruition. It was Kievan art that left to these new centres the grand designs which led to their blossoming in the 12th and 13th centuries. This initial impetus provided a springboard for the most varied forms of artistic expression and a vessel for the interaction of Byzantine art with Russian artistic sensibility.

Novgorod—an independent town

The history of Novgorod follows a course which is quite unlike that of Kiev. Situated at the opposite end to Kiev of the route linking Scandinavia to Byzantium and the Baltic to the Black Sea, Novgorod escaped the Mongol invasion of the 13th century and was thus able to complete its cultural, artistic and economic evolution. This evolution, unlike that of Kiev, bore the stamp of a double influence—the influence both of Byzantium, and of the Germanic world. Thus the economy of Novgorod was entirely founded on commerce, the barren northern soil being hardly suitable for agriculture. Commercial life benefited greatly from the advantageous geographical location of Novgorod on the Volkhov river, which made communications a very straightforward affair and joined Novgorod not only to Byzantium and the Black Sea, but also to the towns of the Hanseatic league (such as Lübeck), and the Baltic. This explains why the Hanseatic towns established so many finance houses at Novgorod. The blossoming of the town was also favoured by its independence relative to Kiev, the most important concrete manifestation of this being in its political institutions. There was no prince at the head of the community, but in his place an elected burgomaster, the *posadnik*, who defended the interests of Novgorod against the prince of Kiev. The town also had a popular assembly, called the *vieche*. In the context of Russia as a whole, Novgorod played the same colonizing role in the north as Kiev in the south. The most enterprising of the merchants accumulated immense fortunes; the Stroganovs, for example, got rich by exploiting the mines in the Urals as well as selling Siberian furs. But in concentrating entirely on trade the citizens of Novgorod neglected to equip themselves with a strong army, and this weakness was the cause of their downfall. As Muscovy grew in stature the tsars, jealous of the wealth and the privileges of Novgorod, began to bear down on them ever more heavily. In 1478 Ivan III suppressed the *posadnik* and disbanded the *vieche*, but from 1495 his incursions took on a more bloodthirsty character: first the Hanseatic finance houses were ransacked, and then in 1570 Ivan the Terrible ordered the town to be sacked and had its citizens drowned in their hundreds in the Volkhov.

While the art of Kiev, like that of Byzantium, impresses by its ostentation and its brilliance, the character of Novgorod is reflected in a simpler and more sober art. The architecture may seem austere at times, but it exhibits elements which are more authentically Russian and which mark its originality compared with Kiev. Neither marble surfaces nor the splendid mosaic of the churches of Kiev are to be found in this northern land. In Novgorod the churches are small and squat, the openings narrower, and the roofs are steeper, influenced by German architecture as well as by the harsher climate. The bays have given way to narrow slits, although the design of these, and their position high up in the walls, permits the cupola to be adequately lit, and even flooded with

The Cathedral of St. Dmitri, Vladimir (1193–1197).

light on fine days. The Byzantine cupola is abandoned in favour of smooth or wood-plated bulbous domes, which permit snow or rainwater to run off, and which are variously disposed—singly or in groups of three (*trekhlavie*) or five (*piatiglavie*). This technique was subsequently adopted in Vladimir, and passed from there to Moscow. Besides this, the first pyramidal steeples are to be found at Novgorod—another idea which reappears in the architecture of Moscow.

One of the most important buildings in Novgorod is the Cathedral of Santa Sophia (1045–1052). Built on a more modest scale than its namesake at Kiev, this cathedral once had three bronze doors, which are evidence of the double influence of Germany and Byzantium. Of these there are only two still in existence—the doors of Sigtuna and Korsun. They bear inscriptions in Latin accompanied by a Russian translation. As in the frescoes and the icons, the subject matter of the bas-reliefs is drawn from both the Old and the New Testament. Of the original frescoes there is unhappily nothing left in any real sense—they were either destroyed or repainted in oil in the course of a quite dreadful attempt at restoration.

There are other buildings from which much can be learned about Novgorodian style; for example, the churches of the monasteries of St. Anthony and St. George (1117–1119), and the Church of the Redeemer on the Nereditsa, built in 1198 and which contains some of the original frescoes. The most beautiful frescoes and icons of ancient Russian art were also created at Novgorod. These masterpieces, often the fruits of collaboration between a number of artists, attain their full maturity in the 14th and 15th centuries. There is a certain uniformity about them which is a result of the restrictions placed upon the subjects that the artists were allowed to treat, and of the guidelines laid down by the code of practice which they observed. The subjects authorized by the church are drawn from the Old and the New Testament and from the lives of the saints. The artist was, however, free to arrange the formal setting as he wished in accordance with his artistic instincts—an area in which the painters from Novgorod excelled.

The province of Novgorod took in several vassal cities, the most important of them being Pskov, which stood at the confluence of two rivers, the Velikaia and the Pskova. As in other places the use of stone, which was in short supply in those parts, is restricted to the churches; the villages were wooden. The architecture of Pskov is similar to that of Novgorod, but not identical. It is characterized by elements that were later adopted in the architecture of other cities: closed exterior galleries, porches, arcades with bays in the steeples. The most important buildings in Pskov are the Church of the Transfiguration in the Spaso-Mirozhski monastery (1156), the Church of St. John the Baptist at the Ivanovski Convent (1240), the Church of Basil the Great (1413) and the 14th century Church of St. Sergius.

The Cathedral of the Dormition, Vladimir (1158–1161), constructed to house the icon of the Virgin of Vladimir.

Vladimir-Suzdal

Subjected to continuous pressure by the nomads, the political centre of ancient Russia was gradually displaced towards the east, and at the beginning of the 12th century was situated in the upper reaches of the Volga. This is a heavily wooded region, well off the Novgorod-Kiev axis—a fact which encouraged commercial and cultural exchanges with Central Asia and the Caucasus and relative independence of Byzantium. Goods were transported on the Volga. Suzdalia maintained close trading links with the Persians, whom they provided with furs in exchange for aromatics, silks, coins and precious stones. The character of the region was rural and there was no large urban centre; two large villages therefore found themselves called upon to play a leading role. These were Suzdal and Vladimir, both founded in the 11th century. It was Andrei Bogoliubski, organizer of the pillage of Kiev, who nominated Vladimir as the first capital of the region. He was all-powerful, because this large village was not equipped with any kind of political structure comparable to that of Novgorod. He dreamed of seeing Vladimir shine with glory as Kiev had once done, and to this end he encouraged the building of numerous churches and civil buildings, such as the Bogoliubovo Palace—the only building of its type and time to have survived to the present day.

The feature which sets the buildings of Suzdalia apart from those of Kiev and Novgorod is the use of white stone in the construction of churches. These are reasonably small, having a single cupola, and they blend well with their environment. Their decoration is individual and concentrates on the exterior surfaces, the well-appointed façades being

prolifically ornamented. Plants, birds, animals and human beings are represented; they are engraved on the flat surfaces, not in relief. The elements are so disposed that the façades have an embroidered appearance. The artistry transcends the subjects. In the buildings of Suzdalia, the Armenian influence outweighs the Byzantine. Apart from the golden gates of Vladimir which date from 1164 and were rebuilt at the end of the 17th century, the most important creations of the architecture of Suzdalia are the following. The Cathedral of the Dormition was built to house the celebrated Virgin of Vladimir (1158–1161). This cathedral was destroyed by a fire in 1183 and later rebuilt. The Church on the Nerl (1165) is the archetypal Suzdalian church: modest in scale, with a single cupola and some finely worked white stone for the upper parts of the building. The well-preserved Cathedral of St. Dmitri, built between 1193 and 1197, exhibits some exceptionally fine ornamentation around the openings and on the drum of the cupola. This is more harmoniously disposed and altogether less exuberant than the ornamentation of the church of St. George in Yuriev-Polskoi (1230–1234).

The Cathedral of the Nativity of the Virgin, Suzdal. In the foreground is a church-isba.

Russia in Peril

Illuminated manuscript of the synodic of the archbishop Afanasi (1689–1690) (Museum of History, Moscow).

Even today, for the Russians the Mongol invasion continues to be a symbol of destruction, horror, domination and terror. It was unleashed on to Russian territory in 1223: towns and forests were burnt, people massacred, artistic and economic life halted. It was a real national tragedy, one which lasted two centuries—two long centuries during which the development of Russia, which had had such a brilliant start, came to a dead stop.

Russia had become the western frontier of the immense Mongol empire. The Russian princes were tributaries of the Golden Horde; in order to keep their hereditary possessions they were obliged to pay tributes and offer valuable gifts to their new masters. The southern regions came off worst: they lost their prince, and from 1249 Kiev was governed by the Mongols.

But great though the ravages and dire the consequence of the Tartar yoke on the cultural and spiritual life of the Russians, their feeling of belonging to a people and a land proved indestructible.

Anxious not to lose their identity during this oppression, the Russians applied themselves to the task of preserving their spiritual and cultural traditions. The political centre of Russia was now displaced northwards into the "Russian Mesopotamia", a triangle formed by three rivers, the Volga, the Oka and the Moskva; and here the town was born which was to control the destiny of Russia until the founding of St. Petersburg— that is, Moscow. It was the Muscovite princes who patiently unified the lands and fought for the independence of Russia. The first milestone on the road to independence was Dmitri Donskoi's victory over the Tartars at Kulikovo in 1380. This marks the start of an irreversible process: in 1389 the khan of the Golden Horde recognized the suzerainty of the grand prince of Moscow over the combined Russian principalities; in 1476 Ivan III refused for the first time to pay the tribute, and in 1480 the Tartars suffered a crushing defeat from which they never recovered.

Throughout this period the Russians were cut off from the regions with which they had links by secular tradition, notably Byzantium. However unfavourable it must have been on an economic level, this situation gave a new impetus to Russian artistic expression. Certainly no new buildings comparable with the cathedrals of Kiev and Novgorod were constructed in the course of these two centuries: men and means were lacking, as were the material and spiritual conditions necessary for the construction of masterpieces such as those. Insecurity encouraged instead the creation of small works of art—small and light enough to be carried easily on the person. There is a whole series of amulets and miniatures dating from this period, as well as icons in a different style (gold being often replaced by brighter colours such as red). Subjects are most often drawn from the lives of saints and martyrs—St. George in the

Left:
"Bread"—a miniature from a 16th-century Russian manuscript (Lenin Library, Moscow).

ⰔⰵⰏꙊⰆⰅⰕⰑⰏⰑⰝⰐⰀⰝⰀⰎⰑⰒⰂⰊⰐⰰ · ⰒⰓⰒⰁ
ⰐⰫⰊⰜⰤⰐⰀⰉⰋⰔⰵⰓⰃⰑⰐⰑꙊⰂⰒⰜⰎⰀⰐⰍⰵ
ⰊⰍⰑꙊⰆⰇⰊⰂⰐⰃⰁⰒⰓⰒⰜⰐⰀⰃⰑⰔⰂⰑⰵⰃⰑ · ⰀⰞ
ⰐⰵⰎⰵⰆⰵⰒⰑⰔⰕⰀⰂⰎⰵⰐⰜⰁⰜⰊⰂⰜⰂⰃⰑꙊⰏⰵⰐⰜⰔⰕⰂ
ⰒⰑⰂⰵⰝⰜⰆⰐⰊⰵⰕⰀⰀⰎⰋⰕⰑⰓⰃⰊⰀⰁⰜⰉⰂⰀⰞⰵ · ⰒⰓⰑ

Miniature (1648) by Antony Siski (Museum of History, Moscow).

13th century, and the prophet Elias (Pskov school). Equally remarkable are the illuminated manuscripts and the products of craftsmanship and applied arts, such as the Ludogochin cross, which dates from 1356.

The artists of Moscow were aware of the heritage of the past, particularly that of Vladimir-Suzdal, and took care to associate their output with the mainstream of culture that came out of it; like the Muscovite princes they fostered a close relationship with Vladimir. It is no coincidence that the earliest Muscovite churches faithfully follow in the architectural traditions of Suzdalia, and are built of white stone. Ivan III sent the architects commissioned to build the Cathedral of the Dormition in Moscow—some of whom were from Pskov, others from Italy—to Vladimir, to study there the architecture of the monuments.

Though sombre and harsh for the Russian people, the period of Mongol domination is thus not lacking in interest as far as the artistic development of the country is concerned. Like the waters of an underground river, the cultural traditions were channelled towards the emergence of Muscovy, where they were recognized and applied. Cut off from their original pole of influence they acquired a more specifically Russian character in the course of this unseen detour.

The man-made habitats are also specifically Russian. In the country, and formerly in the towns also, houses were constructed of wood: stone, being scarce, was reserved for use in churches. Only in northern Russia, above all in the region around Archangel, were the churches also

Right:
In northern Russia, and to a lesser extent in other regions, the isba often formed the starting-point for a church.

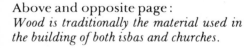

Above and opposite page:
Wood is traditionally the material used in the building of both isbas and churches.

built of wood. It is worth spending some time over these, as they are typically Russian and completely different from Byzantine architecture. Their origin can be traced back to the ubiquitous dwelling-house of rural Russia—the *isba*. This is built from whole tree trunks, the ends of which are trimmed with an axe so that they slot easily together. Any gaps left are filled with moss. Outside the trunks are left rough, complete with bark; inside they are smooth and polished. In general the *isba* consists of one storey only. In this land of intense cold the most important fixture is the stove, around which the inhabitants live. In wealthy houses this may be large and elaborately decorated, and provide not only warmth, but a place to sleep, offering enough space for the entire family to stretch out. The doors and windows are for the most part decorated; in certain *isbas* the wood is so intricately carved that it resembles real lace. In ancient Russia, important complexes of civil buildings were also made of wood—the palaces of the princes of Kiev and the palaces of the Muscovite princes at Kolomenskoi are examples. Visitors from abroad were always struck by the originality of the forms, the tangle of their different parts and the picturesqueness of their many colours. Sadly, they suffered the fate of all the villages of olden times: most often they fell victim to fire, in the course of the tremendous conflagrations that regularly devastated the urban centres of Russia.

Muscovy

Cupolas of the Moscow Kremlin.

Right:
The construction of the citadel of Moscow—the Kremlin—marked the beginning of the irresistible rise of Muscovy.

The emergence of Moscow, which was to become the most important city in Russia, is one of the most significant events in the history of the country. Originally it was just a small market-town founded on the River Moskva by prince Yuri Dolgoruki in 1147. In 1156 the same prince Dolgoruki put up a wooden surrounding wall, by which he transformed the town into a fortress capable of withstanding any attack launched either from Yakhroma or from the river Moskva. The construction of this wooden *kremlin* marks the start of the irresistible rise of Moscow, even though its role was a modest one during the 13th century, being just one of the numerous towns that were threatened or oppressed by the Tartars. It was only in the 14th century, when the political centre of Russia was being pushed northwards, that Moscow assumed the position that was to remain secure for several centuries—that of capital of Russia.

The platform for the political ambitions of the Muscovite princes was rapid economic development in the domain of agriculture, craftsmanship and also commerce, the latter favoured by the geographical situation of Moscow and by the waterways—the Moskva and the Oka—which made possible the transportation of commodities. Moscow maintained mercantile links with Poland, the towns of the Baltic, the White Sea (Archangel) and the Black Sea—in the latter case notably with the Genoese coastal colonies (e.g. at Kaffa)—all of which has an important bearing on the development of Muscovite art. The Muscovite princes patiently reunited the lands, strengthening their new centre, and under the princes Yuri Danilovitch (1303–1325) and Ivan Kalita (1325–1340)

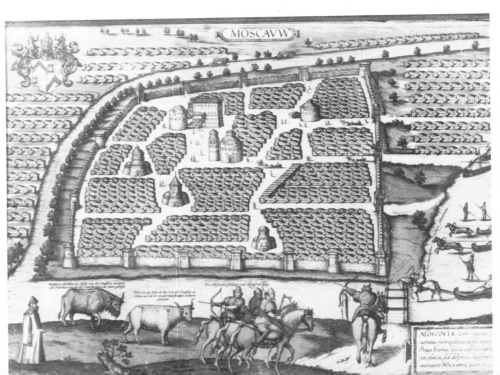

the great Muscovite principality was constituted, forming a strongly centralized state. Moscow was successor to Vladimir on the political and religious levels, the metropolitans establishing their seats there under Ivan Kalita; the rival town of Tver was consigned to obscurity. Demonstrating great political agility, the Muscovite princes maintained good relations with the khans of the Golden Horde right up until the day when, sufficiently strong and well-equipped, they turned on them in a series of battles which eventually led to liberation: Kulikovo in 1380 and the defeat of the khanates of Kazan and Astrakhan in 1552 by Ivan the Terrible. In the meantime Constantinople had fallen into the hands of the Turks, and Moscow thus became the capital of the Orthodox church.

The group of buildings which attracts most attention in Moscow is without doubt that known as the Kremlin*. In the space of less than a century this wooden fortress, erected to protect the prince's palace and the houses of the boyars, was endowed with a marvellous collection of palaces and churches (1475–1509). The Kremlin as we know it today was built in three stages: first the original 14th century wooden *kremlin*,

of which nothing actually remains at all—the majority of the churches such as the Cathedral of the Dormition (1321), the Cathedral of the Archangel (1333) and the Cathedral of the Annunciation (1397) having been reconstructed in later years. Then there is a whole section of the Kremlin that was either built or rebuilt with the help of Italian architects; finally there are the modern buildings.

The Moscow Kremlin is traditionally the political and religious centre of Russia, being the residence of the tsar and patriarch. A large portion of Russian history has been enacted there. There are various reasons why Italian architects were called in for the construction of the buildings: at the time of Mongol oppression Russian architecture had gradually ceased to exist as an art, and when the Muscovite princes wished to resume their traditional role as builders of churches, they

View of the Kremlin from the River Moskva.

* While the term *kremlin* is now generally understood to refer to that in Moscow, it should not be forgotten that many other Russian towns possessed their own stronghold, or *kremlin*, e.g. Nizhni-Novgorod, Novgorod, Pskov, Rostov, etc.

found that they were lacking in experience and their first attempts at building ended in embarrassing failures. There was no choice but to enlist the aid of foreigners. The choice fell upon the Italians, whose reputation for reliability had spread beyond the frontiers of Italy— namely, Aristotile Fioravanti of Bologna, Pietro Antonio Solario of Milan and Alevisio Novi, also of Milan. In addition, in 1472 Ivan III had married Zoë Paleologus, niece of the last emperor of Byzantium: she had been educated at Rome, and she influenced his choice. Eventually, their contacts with Rome superseded those maintained with Greece and Byzantium; among other reasons for this was the presence of numerous Genoese merchants in Kaffa, a town situated on the eastern coast of the Crimea.

The Cathedral of the Dormition (Uspenski Sobor), constructed between 1475 and 1479 under the direction of the Italian architect Aristotile Fioravanti in the centre of the Kremlin, is without doubt one

Above and above right:
The Moscow Cathedral of the Dormition, built between 1475 and 1479.

Right:
The Cathedral of the Annunciation, Moscow (1484–1489).

The interior (left) and the cupolas (below) of the Cathedral of the Annunciation.

of the most imposing monuments of this period. As well as dominating the Kremlin, it was the building that marked the centre of the town under Ivan III. In 1855 Yussef Volozki, a scholar from Kazan, called it "... a terrestrial heaven, shining like a sun on the land of Russia." Like the cathedral in Reims, it was the scene of the coronation ceremonies of the tsars up until the emergence of St. Petersburg.

Before starting work, on the advice of Ivan III, Fioravanti went to Vladimir to study there the Cathedral of the Dormition, which was to serve as a model for that of Moscow. And in fact Fioravanti evidently followed the lines of the cathedral at Vladimir quite closely: for example, in Moscow he makes use of the same façade ornamented halfway up with a row of blind arcades. The walls are of white stone, as in the churches of Suzdalia. The main differences lie in the overall magnitude of the work, the use of pilasters instead of the half-columns used at Vladimir for the ornamentation of the façades, and the single roof covering the entire cathedral.

The Moscow Cathedral of the Dormition impresses with its air of strength, peace and unity. Outwardly this impression is created by the regularity of the building with its five neat cupolas—the wall panels are all made strictly to the same measurements, the height of each one being slightly greater than its width; the semicircle has been systematically used in the gateway, the friezes, the windows and the cupolas. The interior displays the same order and unity: as in a large hall, the eye takes in all of the space, the columns that support the vaults being slender and not obstructing the view. The Moscow Cathedral of the

Above:
The Faceted Palace (1487–1491).

Above right:
The Cathedral of the Archangel Michael (1505–1509) was constructed by Alevisio Novi from Milan.

Dormition stands on a base 3.2 metres (10½ feet) high, and its appearance is quite distinct on account of the fusion of the architectural style of Vladimir with new 'Muscovite' elements. Its iconostasis brings together some of the finest icons of the ancient Russian painters, including the most beautiful masterpieces from Vladimir. The interior was completed in 1574 with a series of frescoes.

Not far away stands the Cathedral of St. Michael the Archangel, built between 1505 and 1509 by the Italian architect Alevisio Novi of Milan. This cathedral blends harmoniously with the rest of the Kremlin churches, although it is of a very different character: the ground-plan resembles that of the Cathedral of the Dormition (five apses and three naves), but the exterior decoration is completely dissimilar—it is both light and expressive, with a marked preponderance of Italian elements; it seems to express a wish to disavow its original purpose, which was to serve as a mausoleum for the tsars. This large and imposing building is capped by five cupolas; its façades, which are divided into two storeys, are ornamented with two rows of pilasters, one above the other. These are surmounted by a moulded cornice—the first time this device is used in Russian architecture. Above this cornice there is a series of scalloped arches bearing the roof. The cathedral is built of red brick, with only certain details—the pilasters and the cornice—being made of white stone. Built in honour of Moscow and its princes, the monument is remarkable for its decorative elements which are very close to contemporary Italian architecture and have little in common with the architecture of Suzdalia.

The small Cathedral of the Annunciation was built not by Italians, but by architects originally from Pskov, and is different again from the two cathedrals described above. Built between 1484 and 1489, it served as a private chapel for the tsars. There are galleries for women, so that they could attend services without having to suffer the indecorous gaze of men. It crouches beneath the palace of the grand prince, and brings together characteristics of the architecture of Pskov and that of Moscow. The interior is particularly noted for the iconostasis, fruit of the labour of Theophanes the Greek and of Andrei Rublev.

The Church of the Laying of Our Lady's Vestments dates from the years 1484–1485, and is notable for a certain type of plan—consisting of a central part dominating the lesser peripheral parts—which served as a model for a great number of churches in the 16th century.

However, the Kremlin, residence of the grand princes and of the tsars, does not consist only of churches and cathedrals. The secular buildings also claim attention, especially the faceted hall—granovitaia palata—built in 1487–1491 by the Italians Marco Ruffo and Pietro Antonio Solario. In this palace, which unfortunately was largely destroyed by fire in 1682, the tsars gave audiences, held the consecration ceremony, and received ambassadors from abroad. Events of historic importance were also celebrated there, such as the taking of Kazan by Ivan the Terrible in 1552. Essentially, the palace consisted of a vast rectangular hall, the vaults of which formed a cross supported at the centre by a single, colossal pillar. The brightly coloured 16th century mural paintings match the vivacious luxuriance of the ceremonial royal costumes, which were embroidered with gold and with precious stones. It is in this hall that the priceless royal silver ware was laid out; and it also housed the throne of the tsar. But the feature which sets this little palace apart from any other building is its exterior design, which accounts for its popular name "many faceted". Adopting a procedure popularized throughout Europe by the Italian Renaissance, the façade is made of blocks trimmed into many small diamond-shaped points.

The Belfry of Ivan the Great dominates the entire group. Built between 1505 and 1508 by Friazine, it was rendered complete in the 16th century by the addition of a steeple. Later, under Boris Godunov, the belfry was surmounted by a gilded cupola, the overall height being then 81 metres (262 feet).

Each building has its own individual features and each deserves to be assessed on its own merits; but, whatever their differences, together they combine to make a coherent and harmonious whole. Even without the buildings which have been added over the centuries, the concentration of secular and religious constructions of the Moscow Kremlin has a strength seldom equalled elsewhere. This relatively restricted space is

Above:
The bell-tower of Ivan the Great. The original tower was built between 1505 and 1508 by Bon Friazin and was rendered complete in the 16th century by the addition of a steeple. Today it reaches a height of 81 metres (262 feet).

Above left:
The Church of the Resurrection (1484–1485).

37

surrounded and protected by walls and watch towers put up between 1485 and 1508 to replace the old wooden fence. Here again the Italian architects have been at work: the round tower of Beklemichev was constructed in 1487 by Marco Ruffo, while Antonio Friazine constructed the secret gate (from which a secret passage led to the river, enabling the tsar to escape in case of danger). The best-known tower is without doubt that of the Saviour (Spasskaia): constructed in 1491 by Pietro Solario and Marco Ruffo, today it still strikes the hour and gives thereby the signal for the relief of the guard. The Kremlin comprises twenty towers in all, five of them being at the gates. The latter are square, whereas the towers at the angles of the walls are round. They are connected by a wall forming a triangle, which was originally surrounded by water on all sides: by the Moskva in the south, the Neglinnaia in the northwest, and on the eastern side by a deep moat excavated between 1508 and 1516. To complete the defence of the Kremlin, two concentric walls were built: that of Kitai Gorod and that of Belizh Gorod.

The Kremlin was the political, spiritual and cultural centre of Russia up until the founding of St. Petersburg. But there were other important centres of religious life—the monasteries. These were both numerous and powerful—Novodievitchi, Donskoi and Spaso-Mirozhski to name but three of them. But it was the Trinity-St. Sergius Lavra that was to become the monastery of monasteries. It was recognized by the church as being the foremost Russian monastery from 1561 onwards.

Yet it is possible to express in words neither its glory nor the faith of the numberless pilgrims who over the centuries, often after having travelled improbable distances, came to kneel and meditate in the Church of the Trinity or the Cathedral of the Dormition of this monastery. Their fervour reflects a faith which has to be shared before the profound significance of the monastery and the spirituality which emanates from it can be appreciated.

Situated about 80 kilometres (50 miles) north of Moscow, it was founded by St. Sergius of Radonezh in 1340. Born in 1314 into a large family from Rostov, he and some of his family settled not far from the site of the future monastery. He became a monk at 23 years of age, and lived the life of a hermit in the forest; he was soon joined by other hermits with whose aid he built the lavra—one of almost thirty monasteries. Word soon began to spread concerning his deeds, his visions and his healing and an ever-expanding crowd of people came to him for advice and consolation. But the role of St. Sergius did not stop at the spiritual: in the political arena he was the figure around whom the Russian princes gathered; he was the author of the greater unity between them, and thus played a contributing part in the strengthening of Muscovy.

In this sense St. Sergius is also a Russian historial figure. He died in 1392 and to begin with was buried in accordance with his wishes in the cemetery of the monastery, although later (in 1422) his relics were placed in a silver sarcophagus set with precious stones and transferred to the Cathedral of the Trinity. The sarcophagus now rests in a room decorated with frescoes and icons painted by Rublev and others.

The lavra continued to fulfil a historical role, even after the death of St. Sergius. It was burnt down by the Mongols in 1408, but was quickly rebuilt and equipped with a wall behind which the tsars and their people sought refuge at the most critical moments in Russian history: for example, in 1608–1610 the lavra held out against a Polish army 30,000 strong. The first of the Romanov tsars, Michael Fedorovich, went there before his coronation, and Peter the Great sought refuge there from the regiments of *streltsy*. Thus the lavra is intimately bound up with the mainstream of Russian history.

Its architecture spans several centuries. While the first stone was laid in 1340, construction work was still going on in the 19th century. Its walls, 1,200 metres (1312 yards) long and in places reaching a height of 15 metres (50 feet), encompass an area that contains what amounts to a miniature city. Both religious and secular buildings are to be found there, differing in style but blending quite well together. There are nine churches and chapels in all, and of these the Cathedral of the Dormition (Uspenski Sobor), built on the orders of Ivan IV and taking the Kremlin cathedral of the same name as model, is the most imposing. Four blue cupolas, studded with gold stars, surround the principal gold cupola. The interior of the cathedral has five apses, and was decorated by the masters of the lavra and those of Yaroslavl. A short distance away stands the Cathedral of the Trinity, which is striking in its simplicity and the purity of its lines. Among the most original of the monastery buildings is the Chapel of the Well, with its twisted blue and yellow columns standing over a sacred spring, to which pilgrims would come in order to slake their thirst. Finally there is the monumental 87-metre (285-foot) bell-tower, built between 1742 and 1769 by Rastrelli and Uchtomski and considered one of the finest in Russia. Secular buildings are also plentiful: the palace of the tsar, dating from the end of the 17th century; the palace of the metropolitan from the end of the 18th; and the refectory in the baroque style built between 1686 and 1692, notable for its faceted frontage in many colours—red, yellow, green and blue. The latter building is also embellished with white columns decorated with plants and clusters of fruit. The interior consists essentially of a large hall, 70 metres (76 yards) in length and richly decorated, used by the metropolitans and the tsars for their receptions.

Magnificent though the architecture of Russia may be, however, it is

St. Sergius of Radonezh (embroidery).

A chalice from Zagorsk (1597).

Cathedral of the Holy Ghost and Cathedral of the Trinity at Zagorsk.

the painting of frescoes and, more important still, of icons that lies at the very centre of Russian artistic expression. This painting is intimately bound up with the life of the Russians and their faith, and represents perhaps the best expression of their artistic sensibility and their identity. It opened out into full bloom at the time of the emergence of Muscovy, although its history goes back to the 11th and 12th centuries, with some genuine masterpieces being produced at Novgorod. The purpose of the icon in ancient Russia was not pictorial like other paintings: its primary function was not to decorate either the church or the home. It served to educate by means of pictorial representation of sacred texts and the dogmas of the church. But above all, the icon was the link between God and man, the agency through which men sent their prayers and supplications: it was like a window that opened on to heaven. An understanding of this is essential if the icons are to be appreciated at their real value: a superficial investigation which ignored this purpose would reveal only the relative uniformity of the subject matter and choice of colours (permissible subjects were described in books produced for painters by the church, and were drawn from the Old and New Testaments and the lives of the saints). A more informed look will uncover in each icon the sensibility of the individual painter, his capacity to find freedom within the formal framework imposed on him, and his striving for refinement and perfection. By his choice of forms and colours and by the attitude of his characters, the painter invests each icon with a life of its own. Geometrical forms are preferred, expressing aspirations towards a spiritual order harmonizing with the real world. The rhythm too is fundamental—the same motif is repeated at regular intervals or alternates with another motif in a strict pattern (rhythm is a particularly important element in the creation of the iconostases). The separation of the outlines of the human figures is also remarkable, the majority of painters having rigorously maintained an exact space between them; so too is the lengthening of the proportions, which results in persons imbued with spirituality seeming to lean towards the celestial. Nature is often represented schematically and relief is absent, the shallowness of the perspective being the consequence of a particular spatial awareness. Russian painting is characterized by the choice of colours as well as of forms. Colour is never an end in itself as it is in modern painting: its properties are exploited solely to give the icon all its expressiveness. It supersedes the word in establishing communication with men, in turn expressing joy, tenderness, sadness, passion or the tragic dimension inherent in all life. The harmony of colours is always observed, even if this means that certain objects have to be coloured in unreal hues (e.g. red mountains, blue horses, etc.). So important is colour in Russian iconography that it can be used to identify the century when an icon was painted and the school to which it belongs. It is one of the elements that give life to a fresco or an icon; it stirs us deeply as we contemplate these, so that the severity of certain forms is forgotten.

What was the technique used in the realization of these masterpieces, and how have the majority of them been able to escape the wear of the centuries and come down to us in all their freshness and their beauty? In the first place it should be noted the techniques of the icon and of the fresco are identical, which, incidentally, explains the fact that the same masters often executed both.

For the icons, a wooden board of either pine or lime served as the support. To this was applied a gesso (plaster of Paris) ground, on to which, when dry, the painter drew his design. It was then coloured with pigments tempered with egg-yolk and extended with *kvass* (rye-beer). In some cases gold-leaf was used; the whole thing was finally coated with a layer of oil-based varnish—the *olifa*—which protected the icon, but which had the undesirable property of darkening very quickly. This goes some way to explaining why for so long the splendour and brilliance of the ancient icons remained hidden, and why the "sadness" of the Russian icons has so often been erroneously mentioned.

43

In the case of the frescoes, the wall was given a layer of plaster, and a first coating of a yellowish colour mixed with straw was applied to this, followed by a brighter coating mixed with cotton. After being coated in this way, the wall was left to dry out. This wall-covering was very resistant, especially on flat surfaces (if the support was curved it was necessary to add fixatives, which oxidized and caused the plaster to deteriorate, damaging the frescoes). For the fresco itself, the figures were sketched in first with a paint-brush. This first rough outline would be carried out by an apprentice. The master would then take over, giving the figures and the faces their definitive forms and expressions. As with the icons, gold and silver-leaf would sometimes be applied on the clothing before the calligrapher arrived to inscribe the names of the saints depicted on the fresco.

The remarkable thing about this is the similarity of the procedures used to prepare the supporting materials for frescoes and for icons; and even more surprising is the fact that icons and frescoes alike are the fruit of team-work, with the exception of only a few major works created exclusively by the master himself.

Icon and fresco-painting in Russia took place at various artistic centres generally known as "schools". There were many of these (Pskov school, Yaroslavl School, Stroganov school, and so on); but three in particular stand out by virtue of the quality and originality of their painting: the Novgorod, Vladimir-Suzdal and Moscow schools—i.e. those at the very centres where Russian architecture had most successfully developed. Each one of these schools, contributing in its own way to the enrichment of Russian painting, gave of its best. The great masters, however, often went to work in different centres: thus works by Theophanes the Greek are to be found in Novgorod as well as Moscow, and those by the master of all Russian painters, Andrei Rublev, in both Moscow and Vladimir. At the present time the majority of icons have been brought together in Moscow, at the Tretiakov Gallery and the Rublev Museum.

The school which produced what are indisputably the finest Russian icons and frescoes is the Novgorod school. And if the architecture of Novgorod produced some remarkably beautiful churches, it still cannot be denied that painting was developed there to an even higher degree. Even before the Mongol occupation there existed at Novgorod numerous workshops where icons and frescoes were produced for the town, and indeed for the entire region. After the submission of Novgorod to the authority of the Muscovite princes, the latter had a great number of the finest masterpieces of the art of Novgorod transported to the capital.

There are some remarkable frescoes dating from this time (i.e. the 12th century); these include the frescoes of Santa Sophia of Novgorod (1144), the Pskov monastery (1156), the Church of St. George in Staraya Ladoga (end of the 12th century) and the Church of the Redeemer on the Nereditsa, near Novgorod (1199). These frescoes are directly descended from Byzantine art, and especially from the art of the mosaic, of which they are the continuation. The two have a number of characteristics in common—the absence of specific national associations, a marked preference for isolated figures, a tendency to employ neutral hues which at first sight seem rather austere. It is precisely this relative simplicity, however, that gives them their great expressive power: to confirm this it is only necessary to contemplate the faces of Piotr Alexandriski and the *prorok* Kya in the Church of the Redeemer on the Nereditsa, those of St. Nicholas, King David and St. George in Staraya Ladoga, and the depictions of the saints in the Blagovechtenenia Church at Arkazhi, near Novgorod. It was also before the 15th century that some of the most beautiful and perfect icons in Russian art were painted in Novgorod. The distinguishing features of these icons, most of which are by unnamed masters, are the concentration of the subject, the repetition of certain lines, and the emphasis placed on the face, particularly the

eyes; examples are the Holy Face, the Annunciation and the Archangel (all from the end of the 12th century), and the Burial (beginning of the 13th). Most of these are now in the Tretiakov Gallery in Moscow.

Afterwards, in the 13th, 14th and 15th centuries, painting in Novgorod underwent a degree of modification: landscapes begin to appear on the icons, blending well with the figures; also, colours become more vivid. Painters begin to use pure hues, with a special liking for bright vermilion. Popular taste dominates, along with traits drawn from folklore. These icons stand out on account of their spontaneity, their ingenuity and their narrative quality.

As far as the frescoes are concerned, the most notable examples are those from the 14th and 15th centuries which are to be found at the Church of the Dormition in Voltovo (1363), the Cathedral of the Dormition in Vladimir (1408), the Church of the Nativity in Novgorod (1390), the Church of the Transfiguration in Novgorod (1378) and the Church of the Redeemer on the Kina (1378). These are closer to 12th century tradition, even though the lines—in particular those of the face—are stronger but less vigorous.

In the 16th century the Novgorod school excelled above all in the very beautiful frescoes at the Therapont Monastery (1500). This monastery is located between Moscow and Archangel, in the forests of the White Lake. It was founded towards the end of the 14th century by two monks, Therapont and Cyril, from the Simonov Convent in Moscow, following the example set by the founder of the Trinity-St. Sergius Lavra; like him they chose to live as hermits. For more than four hundred years this monastery was one of the most active religious centres of northern Russia. Its frescoes were painted in 1500 by Master Dionysius. The monastery is consecrated to the nativity, so the subjects of the frescoes all have something to do with the Virgin. These frescoes are well presented and constitute one of the most important legacies of the Russian cultural heritage. The colours are very fine and very subtle, and strongly evoke feelings of gentleness and tenderness.

The Moscow school of painting rose to prominence during the 16th and 17th centuries, and thus eventually succeeded the Novgorod school. The works of the Muscovite school are quite distinct from those by the masters of Novgorod, both in the subjects treated and in their form: spontaneity and simplicity give way to the quest for a certain sophistication and refinement which are missing from the Byzantine traditions inherited by the Novgorod school. However, this tendency often jeopardizes the straightforward clarity of the work—particularly in the case of the icons: the solitary figure of the Novgorod school is, in Moscow, surrounded by a frieze depicting different episodes from the life of Christ or the saints. This crowding is characteristic of Muscovite painting, as is the use of colours that are more sombre and lustreless than the ones used in Novgorod. To sum it up, there is a lack of spontaneity in the form and of freshness in the colours. Muscovite icons are further from Byzantine tradition; instead there are more authentically Russian features: less transcendental than those of Novgorod, they penetrate further into the reality that is Russia. Local colour is added by means of a more literal representation of landscapes, churches and typically Russian people.

Fresco-painting also enjoyed a dramatic rise in Moscow from the 16th century onwards. Previously, frescoes had usually been carried out by artists summoned to the emergent capital from Novgorod; but by assuming this burden itself, the Muscovite school reinforced in fresco-painting the same trends as in icon-painting. They do, however, display one individual feature not seen in icon-painting, namely the depiction of secular subjects alongside the religious themes, as in the Church of Santa Sophia of Kiev. Frescoes in Moscow are no longer confined to the churches, but are also used for the decoration of civil buildings; an example is the faceted palace, especially the golden room. Episodes from Russian history, the seasons, and even nude and semi-nude figures are depicted there. Among the religious themes it is the Apocalypse which dominates. The frescoes of the Novodievichi Convent (1598) and those of the Moscow Cathedral of the Dormition (1642–1644), on which an entire team of painters was employed, are among the most representative both of this school and this period.

Finally we must consider the works executed at Vladimir-Suzdal, which are sufficiently distinct from the painting of Novgorod to constitute a separate group. The most interesting frescoes of this school are to be found in the Cathedral of St. Dmitri in Vladimir. The central subject is the Last Judgement, created by a Greek painter assisted by Russian artists. The human figures here seem to be more real, this being due to various factors including a certain suppleness of movement. The most popular subject used in Suzdalian icon-painting is the Deësis. On one such icon, painted in the last decade of the 12th century, Christ is depicted between two angels. The format of this icon is unusual, being rectangular; it can be found in the Church of the Dormition in Moscow. In another Deësis, dating from the beginning of the 13th century, Christ is portrayed with the features of Dmitri Solumski, the protector of warriors, who is depicted as himself on a very large icon painted in Vladimir towards the end of the 12th century. Finally there is the icon of the Virgin and Child, with the metropolitan Maxim at her feet; this commemorates the apparition of the Virgin to the latter at the moment when he decided to transfer the seat of the metropolitan from Kiev to Vladimir. The marvellous icon of the Virgin of Vladimir, on the other hand, is not the work of a Russian master: it was painted in Tsargrad (Byzantium) and later removed to Suzdalia by Andrei Bogoliubski. The Suzdalian artists also excelled in the painting of miniatures illustrating old 12th century manuscripts, such as *Hypolitus the Pope of Rome on the subject of the anti-Christ* and the *Evangelical Recitation of Constantin Bolgarski*.

The whole field of fresco and icon-painting bears the stamp of three masters who gave to it a new and exceptional impetus: Theophanes the Greek, Master Dionysius and Andrei Rublev.

Theophanes the Greek, under whom Rublev studied, came originally from Byzantium and settled in Novgorod before moving to Moscow in the second half of the 14th century. He possessed an impeccable mural-painting technique, above all in the choice of predominantly warm-toned colours. A large part of his output has unhappily fallen victim to time and restoration-work; but we can tell from what has come down to us that he was able to impart to his works an emotional depth that had been unknown in Russian art up to that time. He created the frescoes in the Volotovo Cathedral of the Dormition and the Novgorod Cathedral of the Transfiguration—dating from 1378 and unfortunately "restored" —and worked with Rublev to create the first iconostasis in the Cathedral of the Annunciation in Moscow (1405), painting the principal icons of the deësis. This iconostasis played an important role in the development of Russian painting, the individual icons henceforth becoming parts of the whole. Seen from a distance, the icons appear as silhouettes, with a graphic effect that became one of the distinctive features of the Russian icon.

We know practically nothing about the life of the man who was the greatest of all Russian icon-painters, Andrei Rublev. It seems certain that he was born around 1370 and died in 1430; he became a monk at the Spaso-Andronikov Convent, and worked also in the Trinity-St. Sergius Lavra. A pupil of Theophanes the Greek, his work stands out by virtue of its unrivalled perfection. Although it is customary to classify him with the Moscow school, his art reveals nuances that are very close to those of the Novgorod school. Among other works, he created the icons in the Moscow Cathedral of the Annunciation (in which he discarded the austerity of Theophanes and introduced in its place a sense of great gentleness and harmony), and the icon of the Transfiguration; in 1408 he painted the human figures of the Deësis for the iconostasis in the Vladimir Cathedral of the Dormition, and these radiate intense joy and

spirituality. But the greatest of all his masterpieces remains the icon of the Trinity, acknowledged to be one of the most beautiful, if not *the* most beautiful, of all the Russian icons. The three figures which are placed within a circle symbolizing heaven, represent love, friendship and union. The forms are slender and supple, the colours luminous and uncommonly harmonious. The lines are pure and expressive and have much in common with those in the fresco-painting of Novgorod, and are complemented by the vision of an artist whose aim was to portray the soul and not the body.

The case of Master Dionysius is like that of Rublev in that we know little about his life. The first reference to his name occurs in 1470, and it seems probable that he was invited by Ivan III to paint a deësis in the Moscow Cathedral of the Dormition in 1482. It is certain, however, that he was working in Moscow at the end of the 15th century, his art reflecting the opulence and the splendour of the Muscovite court. He was gifted with the ability to communicate the words of the sacred texts in his painting. Many works have been attributed to him, such as the noble and majestic icons of the metropolitans Pierre and Alexis. But his most important work is without doubt the decoration of the Church of the Nativity in the Therapont Monastery, where the scenes portrayed are characterized by the elongated figures and by the expression of joy conveyed by the use of clear, soft colours.

Above and opposite page:
The Trinity, icon by Andrei Rublev dating from the beginning of the 15th century.

Right:
The metropolitan Alexis, icon by Master Dionysius dating from 1462–1483 (Tretiakov Gallery, Moscow).

Ivan the Terrible

Ivan the Terrible; painting by Vasnetsov (1848–1926).

It is impossible to sort out the myth from the reality when the life and reign of Ivan the Terrible are looked at together. His name is associated with the terror by which he ruled and the blood which he caused to be shed—some of it by his own hand. Yet the start of his reign was not inauspicious in that he strengthened the Russian nation; and in achieving this he showed himself to be unusually strong-willed. It was he who liberated Kazan and Astrakhan (in 1552 and 1556 respectively), and thus paved the way for the conquest of Siberia; less than a century later the Russians had reached the Pacific Ocean and founded the town of Okhotsk at a distance of almost 6,440 kilometres (4,000 miles) from Moscow. Besides this, Ivan consolidated relations with the West by sending out diplomatic missions and encouraging economic exchanges, in particular with England and France. The second phase, however, from 1560 to 1584, will always be identified with despotism and terror. Subjugating the towns that had retained their independence, and keeping the wealthiest regions under his personal control, Ivan IV decimated the ancient aristocracy, for which he had conceived a violent hatred. This overturning of the existing structures led to an increase in the strength of bureaucracy and centralism and led to the deaths of thousands of boyars, not to mention the countless victims among ordinary people.

Cultural life was also affected by the ever-increasing subjugation of art to the whims of power. Icon-painting henceforth wears the mantle of officialdom, and becomes further and further removed from Rublev's ideal of attempting to subordinate the rigid prescriptions of the clergy to the inspiration of the artist as regards subject matter. A number of other factors made their mark on Russian cultural life under Ivan IV: the most important of these is the introduction of printing, a century later than in other European countries. The first book to appear was the Acts of the Apostles. Subsequently a manual of good manners (the *Domostrozh*) was published; this was intended for the upper classes, as was the calendar of the Saints completed by the metropolitan Macarius, which was the official Russian calendar until the time of Peter the Great. In the domain of the arts, the stranglehold of the state resulted in a paralysis which was most in evidence in painting: at the beginning of the 17th century, icon-painting entered into a period of slow but intractable agonizing, a victim of the ever increasing expropriation of power and the continuous introduction of new concepts arriving from the west and propagated by foreign artists summoned to the Armoury.

In the field of architecture, the essential feature of the era of Ivan the Terrible is a new tendency to reject monuments of the Byzantine kind, and to substitute buildings in a style derived directly from the wooden architecture of the northernmost regions of Russia. In this way the

Kolomensko—the fortifications and the Church of the Ascension (1530–1532). In this period the national character of Russia was asserting itself in architecture, notably by the tendency to put to use architectural elements originally from the north of Russia, e.g. the tent roof.

national character of the Russians asserts itself, above all in the construction of the churches, although also in secular monuments such as the Kolomenskoi Palace. It is altogether different in conception, even if in the case of certain details (such es the decoration of the porches and the façades) the elements introduced into Russia by the great Italian architects during the preceding period are still in evidence. The most easily identifiable architectural element is the appearance of pyramidal roofs replacing the classical Byzantine cupola; this represents the reproduction in stone of a characteristic element of wooden buildings. It appears very clearly in the construction of the Church of the Ascension at Kolomenskoi (1532) and the Church of the Transfiguration at Ostrovo (1550).

The roof in both of these cases is covered by a single pyramid; also their layout is completely different from that of churches of the Byzantine type—galleries are incorporated, as are large covered stairways, and so on. In the Church of the Nativity in Putinki, Moscow (1649–1652), and the church known as "The Wonder" in Uglich, on the Volga (1628), the architects have preferred to use groups of three pyramids, and this lends some importance to these buildings. But the church that is most representative of the age is that of St. Basil the Blessed, built between 1555 and 1560; this church, all on its own, expresses everything about the architectural and artistic conceptions of the Russian people. This wonderful building, which stands outside the walls of the Kremlin in Red Square, is straight out of some fairy-tale. It is an exceptional monument in many respects, and in fact is not a single church but a combination of several churches. It was built on the orders of Ivan the Terrible. The central part of the building is of stone, with a pyramid roof, and was originally consecrated to the Intercession of the Virgin. It was flanked by seven wooden chapels, each of which commemorated one of the seven saints on whose name-days the Russian army had inflicted a defeat on the Tartars—thus making possible the conquest of Kazan and Astrakhan, and securing deliverance once and for all from the Tartar yoke. These wooden chapels were subsequently rebuilt in brick, and in 1588, on the orders of Feodor Ivanovich, son of Ivan IV, the group was rendered complete by the addition of a new chapel dedicated to "Basil the Innocent", which eventually gave its name to the entire complex. On Palm Sunday, it was to this church that the processions wended their way, with the tsar leading, and holding the bridle of the horse of the Patriarch, who blessed the throng of believers as he passed by.

The Church of St. Basil the Blessed (Vassili Blazhenoi) is remarkable for its impression of harmony and unity, even though the whole is composed of such disparate elements, each of which has its own unique properties. This is especially true of the bulbs—not one of them is like any of the others, neither in its colour nor in its forms (i.e. the sides, the nature of the twisting, the facets, scales, and so on). The interior is sombre and low, and also recalls the wooden churches; their overall gloom is increased by the use of mica in the windows.

But this pyramid form in architecture was to enjoy only a brief interval of glory in the central Russian regions; from 1650 onwards it was forbidden by order of the Orthodox religious hierarchy. Despite this it survived in the more abstruse religions in the north of Russia.

The Church of St. Basil the Blessed in Red Square, Moscow.

The first
of the Romanovs

Ѣздъ Царя Михаила Ѳеодоровича въ Москву. 2 мая 1613 г.

The first tsar of the long dynasty of the Romanovs, Michael Fedorovitch ascended the throne in 1613.

Right:
The Teremnoi Palace is a typical example of 17th-century Russian architecture, where the influence of wood was deeply felt. This building contained the rooms of the tsar.

Following the reign of Ivan IV "the Terrible" there was a period of political, economic and social crisis so profound that in Russian history the name "the Time of Troubles" has persisted. Ivan IV had murdered his elder son by his own hand, and it was the younger who ascended the throne. He was, however, too weak to rule; in 1588 he handed over the reins of power to his brother-in-law Boris Godunov. The latter, officially elected tsar in 1598, found himself ruling a country economically ruined by war and torn to shreds by rivalries among the boyars which had broken out afresh upon the death of Ivan IV. During his reign he strengthened the European outlook of Russia, created an independent patriarchate with Moscow as its seat and did his very best to quell the boyars. But Godunov's authority never assured him of complete mastery over the peasants, whose anger had been mounting since 1580, when measures had been taken to restrict the movement of peasants between employers. Discontent was given momentum by the appalling famines of 1601–1603 and compounded by the epidemics of disease which ravaged the country. Boris Godunov, the "usurper", had to be dethroned. A revolt was organized by Ivan Bolotnikov on behalf of Dmitri, the youngest son of Ivan the Terrible. Godunov let it be known that Dmitri was dead, but rumours began to circulate that he was still alive. So was this the real Dmitri, or a pretender? Even now we cannot be sure. What is certain, however, is that "Dmitri" ascended the throne when Godunov died in 1605. His popularity vanished, however, when he married a Pole, a heretic; he was butchered with 3,000 of his fol-

lowers in 1606. The country was now worn out with fighting, and longed only for peace. In 1613 an assembly consisting of nobles, clergy, merchants and Cossacks elected a new leader—Michael Fedorovich Romanov, who was just 16 years old. He was the first tsar of a dynasty which was to occupy the Russian throne until 1917, and he himself ruled Russia from 1613 to 1645. He was succeeded by Alexis (1645–1676), Theodore (1676–1682) and Sophie (1682–1689). The frontiers of their state no longer ended where Muscovy ended, but extended to form an empire (the formation of the Empire was officially announced in 1721). While it is true that the centralization of political life led to a concentration of artistic life, especially where financially extravagant arts were concerned, in the Kremlin, the fact nevertheless remains that architecture continued to develop throughout the country, particularly in the Volga basin. The number of churches standing increased from 400 at the beginning of the century to 20,000 at its close. In spite of the seizure of political power, and the rift between the old believers and the official church, the latter remained a powerful force in the land.

The imposing Rostov Kremlin, which still stands with its profusion of

The interior decoration of the Faceted Palace, which was destroyed several times by fire, was transformed and renovated by Simon Uchakov in 1658, among others.

Left:
The Trinity, 17th-century icon from Zagorsk. The finest works of art and craftsmanship of the 17th century were executed in the Armoury, Moscow.

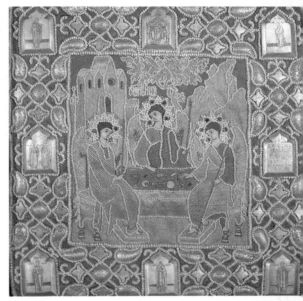

Boris Godunov's gift, embroidery from Zagorsk.

towers and churches with their celebrated carillons, dates from this period. The churches of St. Elias the Prophet, St. John and St. John Chrysostom, all decorated with fine frescoes, were constructed in Yaroslavl. The design that was most widespread in the 17th century was that of the church with five cupolas ornamented with polychrome ceramic, and the church with a detached bell-tower, such as the Church of the Trinity in the place called Nikitniki (1628–1653) and the Church of St. Nicholas in Khamovniki. The 17th century buildings are certainly the monuments of Russian art that are best known abroad. It is also true that buildings such as the churches of Fili (1693–1694), of Ostankino (1670) and those of the Monastery of the New Jerusalem command admiration by their beauty. The pyramid or tent roof, such as was used in the stately church in the Monastery of Alexis in Uglich (1628), was

Above:
Episcopal mitre in gold inlaid with black enamel, set with precious stones and pearls. Zagorsk, 1601.

Above right:
Crown belonging to the full-dress uniform of tsar Michael Fedorovitch.

often the preferred type until it was prohibited by the clergy. Architectural activity reached a new peak within the monasteries also: walls and watch-towers were constructed, as well as churches, civil buildings and bell-towers. Among the best known monasteries, the Trinity-St. Sergius Lavra must receive special mention, as must the Convent of Novodievichi, where the Church of the Transfiguration dates from 1688, its bell-tower from 1690 and the other towers from the 1680s; the Donskoi Monastery, where the church was built between 1684 and 1689, and the Monastery of St. Boris and St. Gleb near Rostov. Even more than in the preceding centuries, the emphasis is on the decoration of the exterior walls—not only in religious constructions, but in civil buildings also. One of the most astonishing of civil buildings was the Kolomenskoi Palace, erected in 1667–1668 and modified in 1681, and of which unhappily no records remain except in some engravings. Strictly speaking this was not a single building but a lot of buildings jumbled together, intercommunicating by passages and galleries forming a small town that was more like the stage sets for an opera than real life. This

Above:
Silver plate. The Armoury, 1649.

Left:
Silver table ware. The Armoury, 1618.

impression was compounded by the profusion of the decoration, the colours and the roofs—of which no two were alike (there were pyramids, bulbous domes of various kinds, and so on). In Moscow, within the Kremlin itself, two civil buildings were constructed: the Teremnoi Palace (1635) and the Palace of Amusements (1652).

The Teremnoi Palace, erected on the foundations of an old building dating from the time of Vassili III and Ivan IV, housed the rooms of the tsar. Access is by means of a fine stone staircase which leads to a flight of steps known as the "golden perron"—in former times it was, of course, lavishly decorated with paintings and sculptures. The first room is equipped with magnificent faience tiles of Dutch origin, and was reserved for the boyars who waited there for the arrival of the tsar. It was in the second room—the Salon—that the tsar gave audiences and on occasion received foreign ambassadors. The third room was the tsar's study, and was called the throne-room. The most beautiful room in the Teremnoi Palace, in the 17th century it was barred to everyone except the intimate friends of the tsar. A box used to be lowered from one of the windows, and anyone could place in this their petitions or grievances addressed to the tsar (but which in general went unanswered). Access to the tsar's bedchamber was restricted to members of the imperial family.

Above:
Embroidery. Zagorsk, end of the 16th century.

Above right:
Coach belonging to Catherine II; it seated four persons, and was used for official engagements. It was built in England in 1769, and decorated by painters of the Watteau school.

This chamber communicated with the oratory, where the tsar prayed morning and evening. In the 17th century the decoration of the interior of the palace was entrusted to Simon Uchakov, one of the last icon-painters to be known in Russia. The windows were of multicoloured mica, and cast a strange other-wordly light on to the red velvet-upholstered furniture and the chests filled with jewels and gold and silver ware. In 1637 a new and spacious room was added to this complex: called the *teremok*, its windows and door are elaborately sculpted. The richness of this decoration seems to recall that of the churches of St. Dmitri in Vladimir and St. George of Yuriev-Polskoi.

The Palace of Amusements was constructed in 1652 for a member of the tsar's family, and was converted into a theatre in 1679. Performances of every sort were put on there for the imperial family. As time went by, frequent alterations were carried out to all but the central part of the palace; this part has, however, come down to us unchanged, and thus provides information about the state of development of civil architecture in the 17th century. As in the Teremnoi Palace, the door and window frames are elaborately carved. Formerly there was a chapel on the upper storey of the palace, with an altar supported by overhanging arcades.

It is clear that, generally speaking, architecture in 17th-century Moscow, whether civil or religious, was becoming increasingly dissociated from foreign influences, both Byzantine and European. A national character began to develop instead—a trend which was brought back into the public consciousness in the 18th century by Peter the Great's policy of westernization and its realization by European architects.

In the 17th century the main concentration of arts and craftsmanship was in Moscow, more especially at the Armoury, a palace in the Kremlin. The origins of this palace go back to the 14th century, when the treasure of the grand princes of Moscow came into being; this was augmented over the years until eventually, in the 15th century, a separate building was required in order to house it. However, it was not until the 16th century that these treasures were deposited at the Armoury. In the 17th century this same palace became the centre for arts and craft skills in Russia: the best armourers, jewellers, gold and silversmiths, potters and icon-painters came together here from the farthest corners of Russia and abroad, to create in their individual fields the works of art that were rightly the pride of the Russian court.

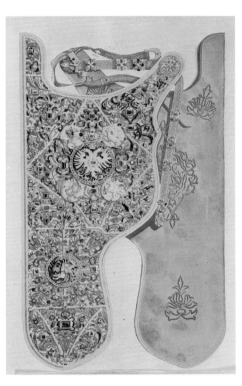

Saddle belonging to Peter I. The Armoury, Moscow.

Silver candlestick. Zagorsk, 1601.

Detail of the wooden "hollow candle" (1664), from the Church of the Transfiguration by Friazine (Vologola District Museum).

The armourers of the 17th century were contributing to the enlargement of a collection of arms that was already antique: the most ancient piece—the helmet of Yaroslav Vsevolodovich, father of Alexander Nevski—dates from the beginning of the 13th century. The objects on show in this section of the Armoury thus permit us to follow the course of Russian military history from its earliest beginnings up to the formation of the regular army in the 18th century. Russian weapons were not only very effective—although often rather heavy—but were also pieces of skilled metal work, especially those reserved for the use of the tsar and the boyars at important ceremonies. Where their predecessors had used gold, silver and precious stones to adorn the coats of mail belonging to the grand princes and tsars (Boris Godunov's coat of mail is an example), the armourers of the 17th century applied themselves to the sumptuous decoration of cold steel, firearms and daggers, encrusting the golden hilts and scabbards with precious stones such as rubies, emeralds and sapphires. Mother-of-pearl and ivory were used to embellish the stocks of guns with barrels of embossed gold. The hunting guns used by the 17th century tsars—and those which later belonged to Peter I—are among the finest pieces in the collection.

Russian gold and silver has always amazed foreign visitors by its fabulous richness, whether the pieces concerned belong to the court and the boyars or to the churches and monasteries: goblets, bowls and chalices, communion plates, stars, censers, crosses, covers for the gospels and the embellishment of icons. As in the other divisions of Russian art, the double influence of the east and the west made itself felt in the conception of these pieces. In the 17th century, luxury and a highly ornamented style became a particularly strong trend. Table-ware compelled attention by virtue of its elegant forms, perfectly set off by an engraved decoration, or by one of polychrome enamel or gemstones. From the middle of the 17th century a clear preference for bright and bold colours emerged while the use of enamel, with its decorative and pictorial qualities, became widespread (especially bright green translucent enamel associated with emeralds and rubies): an example of this is the chalice given by the patriarch Nikon in 1653 to tsar Alexei Mikhailovich. The embellishment of icons became standard practice, with adornments of gold and precious stones covering the entire painted surface except for the face and hands.

As the years went by, and the master goldsmiths and silversmiths developed more and more refined techniques, their ornamentation became more and more exuberant until by the end of the century there was hardly a surface left anywhere that was not decorated. Their themes were drawn from biblical and mythological subjects as well as from folklore, elaborated with stylized plants and scrolls.

Running parallel to this luxurious extravagance and to that of the precious enamelling on gold a more discreet form of enamelling—mostly in whites and greens—with silver filigree-work began to spread at around the end of the century. Taken together these pieces form a unique group; and most of them testify to the blossoming of the luxurious arts in 17th century Russia, in the wake of the considerable economic, political and cultural advances in the country. Court ceremonies, no less sumptuous than those of the church, stimulated demand for ever greater luxury; gold and silversmiths put all their imagination into the creation of masterpieces so magnificent that any one of them was fit to be used as a symbol of political or religious power. They were exceptional pieces by any standards, and all the more so on account of the easy blending of Russian tradition with the new influences coming in from the west.

Silk and brocade were hardly produced at all in Russia before the time of Peter the Great, and so these fabrics were imported from the east or the west. Until the 15th century they came mostly from Byzantium. From the 16th century to the middle of the 17th, Italian textiles were favoured, as in the stole of the metropolitan Makarios (1543–1564); these were superseded in turn by French materials, which were especially

Left:
The Novodievichi Monastery, founded in Moscow in 1524.

Below:
The Rostov Kremlin: second half of the 17th century.

Belonging to the mainstream of north Russian architectural tradition, the churches of Kizhi exhibit a marvellously harmonious cohesion.

well liked for their light weight. But the element that gave to these fabrics their value was the embroidery with which they were decorated. Often executed in silver or gold thread, this consisted of complicated and richly fantastic designs. They were set off by precious stones and by pearls, the latter being a special feature of the ornamentation of Russian ceremonial dress.

As with gold and silver ware, it was in the 17th century that the most sumptuous embroidery was created: real river pearls and large sea pearls, arranged in branches, twigs and leaves, covered the fabric of mitres, phelonions, stoles and altar-cloths: an example is the phelonion offered by the tsar Fedor Mikhailovich to the Novospasski Convent. The so-called Godunov school produced some of the greatest works of art of the century. Embroidery was also employed in the making of icons, as in the 17th-century icon of the Virgin and Child, which is embroidered entirely in gold thread except for the faces and the hands.

No less sumptuous are the saddles and the harnessing which, like the gold and silver ware, were used in the glittering court ceremonies. Their most glorious period was around the middle of the 17th century, when the Russian army was expanding rapidly and as many as 16,000 people made up the baggage trains, with 150 horses in the tsar's train alone (not to mention those of the tsarina, the diplomats and others). Numerous gifts were sent from abroad (Poland, Germany, Persia, Turkey) to the Russian court, and the ostentation and variety of these was unrivalled except by Russian produce—bits, breast-pieces and saddles, lavishly damascened, ornamented with enamel on gold or silver or studded with precious stones. An example is the saddle of tsar Michael Romanov which was adorned with diamonds, sapphires, rubies and emeralds.

The Russian coach-builders of the 17th century produced a number of fine carriages, both on wheels and on runners—the latter facilitating transport in the long hard winters—but the majority of commissions for the court went abroad. Austrian, German and Polish coaches were ordered (the first coach with mica windows was Polish); but English and French coaches, especially those from the workshops of Buckindal and the Parisian coach-builder Bournihall, were most highly prized.

Kizhi

While the evolution of Russian art was destined to reach a very important turning-point in St. Petersburg, at the beginning of the 18th century the Russian architecture *par excellence*—that is, architecture in wood—enjoyed a second heyday, especially in northern Russia. Wooden churches as remarkable as those of St. Joachim and St. Anne in Morzhegora, near Archangel, the church of Vitegorsk in the Vologda region (1708), that of St. Nicholas near Yaroslavl, and the Church of the Trinity, again near Archangel, were constructed at this time. But the finest and most accomplished of all is the Church of the Transfiguration in Kizhi, built in 1714 on the banks of Lake Onega. Its 22 cupolas are wonderfully complemented by the surrounding landscape. Like the Church of St. Basil the Blessed in Moscow, this very complex building radiates an impression of perfect harmony. The exuberance of the roof makes an arresting contrast with the simplicity of the walls that bear it. This building, the only one of its kind, was completed in 1764 by the addition of the Pokrovskaia church, with its 9 cupolas, and of a belfry. These elements form a whole the beauty of which has no equal other than its own reflection in the waters of Lake Onega. Kizhi may be considered the culmination of that Russian style of architecture which, in the 17th century, had succeeded in breaking away from the Byzantine model and flourishing from a basis that was authentically Russian, in terms both of form and of the material in use.

The Church of the Transfiguration, Kizhi.
The scales of the domes are of wood.

The Westernization of Russia

Peter I, who founded St. Petersburg at the beginning of the 18th century: this town was to be the "window open on the west".

While the 17th century had been marked by the reaffirmation of Russian political and economic power, and artistic expression had acquired a more specifically national character, at the beginning of the 18th century we witness a complete and profound reorientation which has often been attributed to the will and tenacity of one man—Peter I. In reality this is the culmination of a new current which had carried a number of boyars more or less openly along with it, and had even been heeded by the tsar himself in the 17th century. In fact, the new direction in which Russian art and architecture were steered at the beginning of the 18th century, however radical it might appear, did not simply spring up without warning, to put a stop to the nationalist tendencies of the previous century. It was the fruit of the closer and closer links which Russia maintained at various levels with foreign powers in the course of the 17th century. To begin with, commercial relations with various European countries were stepped up thanks to the opening of the port of Archangel, which offered more direct access to Russian markets. These markets were of interest to France and England particularly; the Germans, for their part, sought to establish firmer links with Moscow in order to gain a more direct passage through to Persia and India. This new commercial highway brought an ever-increasing number of foreigners pouring into Moscow. At first they settled inside the town, but the xenophobia shown by the local inhabitants, and even more by the clergy, who took a very dim view of this rising tide of heretics in the

Right:
The Fortress of St. Peter and St. Paul was founded on 16 May, 1703: this date marks the start of work on St. Petersburg.

capital, forced them to establish themselves in a district set aside for them on the approaches to the town (the nemetskaia sloboda). But this relegation for foreigners to the outside of the town had an opposite effect to what was anticipated: the new district exerted a growing influence over the more open minds of Muscovy and held an increasing fascination for them, and it was precisely here that Peter the Great first came into contact with the European way of life.

In spite of resistance from the Slavophiles, those in high places became progressively more westernized: the households of the great boyars were run in the western manner, and more and more foreign artists were summoned to the Armoury. Under their influence painting became secularized: disregarding the models stipulated by the clergy, Russian painters took western painting as their example, producing portraits and showing a proclivity for engraving. Simon Uchakov, who decorated the Teremnoi Palace and also worked in the Trinity-St. Sergius Lavra, typifies this period of transition. The influence of the west was further reinforced by the annexation of Little Russia—the Ukraine—which had been deeply affected by the culture of Poland.

Catherine II, who favoured a classical approach in the architecture of St. Petersburg. This tendency was predominant with a few slight differences for nearly a century, and had a profound effect on the overall appearance of St. Petersburg.

Left:
The canals of Leningrad. The town was built upon the northern marshes, and was drained by a network of canals which earned it the name "Venice of the North".

The Winter Palace, constructed between the years 1754 and 1762 by Rastrelli, who embodied the Russian rococo style. His monumental façades exhibit a certain weightiness in spite of the richness of their decoration.

The growing commitment to western culture of people who held high office at the end of the 17th century created a favourable climate for the reforms of Peter the Great, at the same time as paving the way for the profound division which separated Russian aristocrats, intellectuals and artists from the great majority of the Russian people, who neither would nor could follow this path.

The history of Russia in the 18th century bears the unmistakable stamp of the politics and the personality of those who occupied the throne for the longest periods—namely, Peter I, the Empress Elizabeth and Catherine II. Thoroughly versed in western culture and philosophy, they made great efforts to push the development of Russia in the same direction and the 18th century was, for Russia, the century of Enlightenment. The chief author of this development was Peter I (1700–1725). Guided principally by the idea of a strong state, he governed with very little regard for the respect of his people, and this led to serious rebellions in spite of the progress that the country was making.

In St. Petersburg, the canals are every-where.

The background to his cultural politics was provided by the rapid expansion of the country. This was first and foremost a territorial expansion, made possible by the formation of a regular army 100,000 strong which succeeded both in keeping open access routes to both the Black Sea and the Baltic and in conquering large areas of the Baltic countries (Estonia and Latvia) as well as sustaining the protectorate of Russia over Poland. This expansion was supported by rapid economic development: the number of factories quickly increased, Russian metallurgy was foremost in the world (notably the Demidov factories in the Urals) and the textile industry gained a firm foothold in the regions around Moscow and Vladimir. In order to encourage manufacturers, the state granted them privileges hitherto reserved for the nobility, notably the right to own serfs (which led to the formation of a new category of factory serfs). And last, in the course of the 18th century, Russia began to take a more active interest in European politics. Peter I, who had come into contact with the European way of life in the foreign quarter of Moscow, completed this education by making two voyages abroad. The first was in 1697—he embarked upon it incognito—and was cut short by the revolt of the streltsy, whose ring-leaders he executed on his return; the second took place in 1716, and while travelling he personally engaged a host of artists, master craftsmen and workers who were to help in the construction of St. Petersburg. The "Petersburg Baroque" style dominated architectural activity under Peter I.

Totally committed to the west, Peter I did his best to break with Muscovite traditions. The success of the reforms he pushed through was variable, and they were not accepted without difficulty: he had the beards of the boyars cut by force, ordered German or Hungarian dress to be substituted for the Russian, and introduced a new calendar. He was impatient to watch "his" town expanding, and forbade the use of stone in building throughout the rest of the country on pain of exile and confiscation of goods—the purpose of this being to draw masons and other newly unemployed artisans to St. Petersburg.

After his death in 1725, the throne passed through various hands, but none of his immediate successors was able to last for more than 2–3 years. Not until 1741 did Elizabeth, daughter of Peter I, come to power, and there she stayed until 1762. Brought to the throne of Russia by the nobility, she made it her business throughout her reign to support and strengthen them: thus only noblemen were permitted to possess populated land, had the authority to deport transgressors to Siberia and to choose the governors of districts; finally, they no longer had to fear the freeing of serfs who volunteered for the army, Elizabeth having annulled a decree of Peter I in this respect. An aristocracy grew up that consisted of major landowners, who might possess tens of thousands of serfs— sometimes the empress herself even made over gifts consisting of thousands of serfs. In order to advance the economy, Elizabeth abolished internal customs and set up banks. The Russian army won some battles, notably in eastern Prussia. These newly acquired territories were, however, given back to Prussia by Peter III, who succeeded Elizabeth in 1762. A fervent admirer of Frederic II, he scarcely had time enough to work out a new political direction for the country: he was dead within a few months, strangled on the orders of his wife, Catherine II. Of German origin, Catherine made strenuous efforts to get to know the country which she was to govern for the next 34 years (1762–1796). She travelled extensively to familiarize herself with Russian traditions and their way of life. Liberal in appearance and inspiration—she corresponded with Voltaire and was an admirer of Montesquieu—she nevertheless governed her country with an iron fist. Serfs became more numerous; the privileges of the aristocracy remained intact. A rebellion instigated by Pugachev, bringing together serfs, Cossacks and others, persuaded her to embark upon a programme of reforms, backed up by the advice of Potemkin, her lover and mentor for 13 years. She carried out a degree of decentralization and fixed the rights and duties of every social class. Being both intellectual and a woman of action—these qualities compounded by a turbulent emotional life—she remains one of the great figures of Russian history. In artistic matters her preference was for classicism, and this left a more profound and enduring mark upon Russian architecture than the rococo style favoured by Elizabeth. Classicism was the dominant style in Russia for nearly a century, and was a formative influence on the architecture of St. Petersburg.

The cultural life of the 18th century as a whole is marked by various events of importance, especially where the Russian language is concerned. In 1708 Peter I had replaced the 43-character Slavonic alphabet with a 36-character alphabet that more closely resembled Latin. A literary language gradually began to evolve, the grammatical framework of which was established by the scholar Lomonosov. After a period of supremacy, the foreign masters of the universities founded at St. Petersburg and Moscow made way for Russian scholars and academics. The first signs of a system of universal education began to appear, and a

It was Falconet, a Frenchman, who executed this imposing statue of Peter I: one of the symbols of the town of Leningrad, it was inaugurated in 1782.

Opposite page:
The fountains of the Peterhof (Summer Palace).

number of institutes were set up for noble families: an example is the Smolny Institute, which was founded by Catherine II for the daughters of noblemen. In the realm of history, for the first time interest began to be shown in the past, and it was in the course of this century that the first written account of Russian history was published. Science was enriched by the translation of foreign textbooks on geometry, physics, anatomy, and so on. The Academy published an atlas. Drama began to attract interest, centred on new theatres established in St. Petersburg, Moscow and Yaroslavl.

The 18th century also witnessed the arrival of great writers—the poet Derzhavin, Fon-Vizin, Krylov, Karamsin. But authority, however enlightened it was, could not tolerate any criticism. The writer Radishchev, in his *Journey from St. Petersburg to Moscow*, concentrated on the iniquities of serfdom, and was exiled.

Peter I also attempted to curb the power of the church. He took more control of ecclesiastical procedures and replaced the patriarch with a college of 9 members, the Holy Synod (1721). The church's possessions were administrated thereafter by an economic college, which consisted

The Peterhof (Summer Palace). The empress Elizabeth engaged Rastrelli to refurbish the modest Summer Palace of Peter I. The present-day building dates from 1747–1752, and reflects the tastes of the period.

of lay members. All these upheavals, however, made little impression on the Russian people, whose traditions and customs remained virtually unaltered until they were rediscovered on the intellectual and artistic plane in the course of the 19th century.

The politics of art under Peter I and after had consequences that were profound and important. A radical break with the past took place, and the influence of the West became all-important. Apart from this, where there had been various different cultural centres before, art in all its forms now became concentrated in a single place—St. Petersburg—and the centralization of art was absolute. This new direction also broke up the unity that had existed previously, when art had been aimed at all people. Henceforth there was a deep division between the new western-

ized art which was produced essentially for the aristocracy, and popular art directed towards the great majority of the people. The latter rejected this predominantly secular art, which, being foreign in its conception and expression, was beyond their comprehension. Early on it bore the marks of Dutch influence above all, but this later gave way to French influence. This was particularly true in the fields of architecture (the architects Le Blond and Vallin de la Mothe came to work in St. Petersburg), sculpture (Gillet and Falconnet) and painting (Le Lorrain). Italian influence was also formative, especially in architecture: the Italians Trezzini, Rastrelli and Quarenghi helped to shape the profile of the town with a very large number of buildings. St. Petersburg is indebted to them for its most impressive and original constructions.

The site chosen by Peter I for the founding of "his" capital may at first sight seem rather strange. While Moscow is situated in the heart of the country, St. Petersburg lies in a far-flung corner of northern Russia. The estuary of the Neva is an inhospitable area: the climate there is harsh and foggy, and the landscape barren. The "window on Europe" opens on to a disinherited region, entirely flat and consisting mainly of swamps as far as the eye can see. The location is, however, favourable from a strategic angle. Militarily speaking, it makes possible the defence of Russia against invasion from the north. From a commercial angle, St. Petersburg took business away from Archangel and eventually became Russia's leading maritime port.

The construction of the town was subject to very rigorous controls, in accordance with the ideas of Peter I: the streets were made broad and straight, the façades of the houses were to give on to the street and not on to a courtyard, and the height of all buildings was fixed. In order quickly to populate the town, every boyar was obliged to build a house there, the dimensions of which would be dictated by the number of souls he possessed. Unity and harmony were the key words in the construction of the town, which, unlike Moscow, was to be built entirely of stone (although the very first buildings were of wood). Under Peter I, the style of buildings was quite restrained, as much in civil as in religious architecture. Petrovian architecture is customarily classified with Baroque art.

Peter the Great's primary objective was to build on the swamps a town that would be entirely different from Moscow—that would earn the title of "the Venice of the North" on account of the myriad reflections of its beauty in the Neva and its numberless canals—the Moika, the Fontanka, and the rest.

The Fortress of St. Peter and St. Paul, built on an island in the Neva, was the first of the buildings of the new capital to be constructed. It is a reminder of one of the main purposes of the town—namely, to defend the Baltic seaboard against attack. Work began on the 16th May 1703; later, between the years 1712 and 1733, a monumental cathedral was added—the Cathedral of St. Peter and St. Paul. The layout of this edifice is quite different from the traditional canon of Russian architecture, comprising as it does a basilica with three naves. The decoration was primitive, but was altered after part of the building was damaged by fire in 1756. The cathedral is the work of one of the numerous Italian architects working in St. Petersburg, D. Trezzini. The cathedral seems to

Detail of the church of Tsarskoe Selo, completed in 1738.

Right:
Rastrelli's "Grotto" (1755–1762). The empress Elizabeth hoped to turn Tsarskoe Selo into a "Russian Versailles".

Tsarskoe Selo, the preferred abode of Elizabeth.

lack co-ordination overall, its most impressive part being the monumental spire of its gigantic belfry, the 34 gilded metres (111 feet) of which soar up into the sky above St. Petersburg; this is the most prominent feature of the profile of the city, which it governs in the same way as a cathedral such as that at Strasbourg dominates the whole town. Peter the Great was determined that this belfry should be higher than the one built by Ivan the Great in the Moscow Kremlin. The spire which tops it instead of the Byzantine cupola takes the form of a sharp-pointed pyramid—the first appearance of this in Russian architecture. This is one of the main distinguishing characteristics of the architecture of St. Petersburg. This cathedral was to be tomb of the tsars of Russia who, incidentally, would have seen their last resting place daily from the windows of the Winter Palace during the St. Petersburg period. Previously, in pre-St. Petersburg times, this function had been performed by the Cathedral of the Archangel Michael in Moscow.

Shortly after the construction of the Fortress of St. Peter and St. Paul, a second fortress, the Admiralty, was built on the left bank of the Neva. Around this building lay the Basil Island district which was later to become the centre of the capital, and from which the town's three great highways diverge—the Nevski Prospect, the future Voznesenski Prospect and the Gorokhovaia Prospect. The original edifice was surrounded by moats and fortifications and defended by drawbridges; but it was altered between 1806 and 1823 to the form which is familiar today—that of a fine Empire building. These modifications were the work of the Russian architect Zakharov, who, among other projects, had worked on the designs for the Arc de Triomphe in Paris. Under Peter I, Trezzini directed the construction of other buildings which helped to form the image of St. Petersburg: the Building of the Twelve Colleges (1722–1733), and the St. Alexander Nevski Lavra. The former housed the Senate, the Synod and ten colleges, and is remarkable for its simplicity and rationality: here all the departments of government were brought together under a single roof, although each was able to retain its

Above and above right:
The amber room and Chinese room at Tsarskoe Selo.

independence. The St. Alexander Nevski Lavra, the plans for which were regrettably altered by Trezzini's successor, should have equalled or even surpassed the Trinity-St. Sergius Lavra near Moscow in both its dimensions and its beauty.

When Elizabeth succeeded her father to the throne, her preference was for the rococo style, the Russian incarnation of which was perfectly represented by the buildings of Rastrelli; it also reflects Elizabeth's weakness for pageantry, luxury and great festivities in sumptuous settings. Examples of this are the Winter and Summer Palaces, the palace of Tsarskoe Selo and the Smolny Monastery.

The Winter Palace of St. Petersburg was built between 1754 and 1762 by the Italian Bartolomeo Rastrelli—the most productive architect of 18th century Russia. Indeed, Rastrelli's designs are numerous, not just in St. Petersburg but throughout Russia: e.g. St. Andrei's Church in Kiev (1747–1762), the Church of the Smolny Convent (1748–1757), the transformation of the Peterhof Summer Palace (1747–1752), the palace of the Stroganovs (1750–1754) and the Tsarskoe Selo Palace (1752–1756), to name but a few. In 1730 Rastrelli, who was to perfect the Russian rococo style, was summoned by Elizabeth to the court of Russia, where he remained principal architect throughout her reign.

The Winter Palace was Rastrelli's last great work; its sheer size is even more imposing than its beauty, and it dwarfs the Fortress of St. Peter and St. Paul which stands opposite. It consists of four monumental wings surrounding a central cross-shaped area. Its four façades face the Neva, the Admiralty, and the two neighbouring squares. A mile and a quarter in length and originally painted dark red, it is still overpowering, despite the plentiful ornamentation of Ionian and Corinthian columns (arranged in two rows, one above the other) and the numerous statues high up on the building. The cost of this construction was a relatively modest

2.5 million roubles, and it contained 1,000 rooms and halls; but it was too great an undertaking to complete in Elizabeth's reign, and had to be finished under Catherine II, after Rastrelli's death. The interior was completely renovated after the fire of 1837.

But one single palace was definitely not enough for Elizabeth. She decided to refurbish the summer residence of Peter I, the Peterhof, which had been the work of a number of architects, including the Frenchman Le Blond. Modest in scale and presentation, it was completed and entirely renovated by Rastrelli in the years 1747–1752.

In fact, architecture and the arts found themselves looking on while the power of the monarchy became stronger and the court of Russia more refined—the latter process having been considerably accelerated since the founding of St. Petersburg. Rastrelli retained the basic plan—a central part flanked by two lateral wings—although he added a third storey to the central part. He also changed the cupolas of the pavilions adjoining the wings. As at Smolny, the church was given the traditional five cupolas of Russian architecture. However, the interior disposition of the Peterhof was completely reorganized. The great staircase was moved from the centre towards one side, where it opened on to a row of salons and ceremonial rooms, as at Tsarskoe Selo. To call the decoration exuberant would be an understatement: there is a profusion of colours, gilding, garlands, sculptures and paintings. Everywhere there is vivacity and movement, right up to the mirrors reflecting the splendour which provided a background for the court celebrations. Equally exuberant is the spectacle of the fountains. The idea for these came originally from Peter I. Beneath the castle, surrounded by water, there is a cave. The water falls on to the steps of a large stairway, then descends into a pool. On each step there are statues, from which the water also issues. At the centre of the large pool, the edges of which are adorned by sirens, tritons and other mythological figures, there is a representation of Samson forcing open the mouth of a lion. This impressive statue stands on a pedestal that consists of a rock. From the mouth of the lion a jet of water gushes to a height of 60 metres (c. 200 feet). The waters of the large pool are then drained away to the sea by a long straight canal bordered by fountains. There are other fountains in the grounds, which descend gently towards the Gulf of Finland.

But Elizabeth's preferred palace was that of Tsarskoe Selo, and under her reign this became one of the official residences of the tsars. The original building which grew into this imposing palace was a small construction dating from 1722, standing on a wooded inland hill. Such a modest construction was quite inadequate to satisfy Elizabeth's taste for ostentation, and as soon as she came to power Tsarskoe Selo erupted into feverish activity. Whole villages had to be constructed for the workers and craftsmen who were to be entrusted with the redevelopment of the palace. First to be built was a stone church, which was completed in 1738. But despite the many sets of plans drawn up and the building work undertaken by the architects who preceded Rastrelli, Elizabeth was never satisfied, and her demands for modifications were incessant. Then in 1752, on the orders of the empress, Rastrelli decided to design an entirely new and majestic group of buildings—a "Russian Versailles" as Lomonosov admiringly called it. He matched the height of the existing buildings and created a palace of colossal dimensions—300 metres (330 yards) long, flanked on both left and right sides by two symmetrical cupolas. The uniformity of the façades and of the overall proportions was balanced by a great variety of columns, pilasters, colours, window decorations and by a range of gilded statues and urns on the balustrade. The precisely laid out park was adorned with pavilions for the use of those out walking or hunting; the most notable of these pavilions were the Monbijou and the Hermitage, together with the Grotto situated on the large lake. Inside the palace, the great staircase gave access to two impressive suites of chambers, the more imposing of which—the "great hall"—extended from one exterior wall to the other. This hall, following the example of the gallery of mirrors at Versailles, was decorated entirely with mirrors, which in fairy-tale fashion reflected back the light of the 695 candles in 56 chandeliers serving to illuminate the hall for all great occasions. Also of note is the Chinese room, which, as its name suggests, was decorated with the Chinese themes that were so very fashionable at the time. The amber room is remarkable for the amber plates adorning its walls, given to Peter the Great by Frederick William I, king of Prussia. The picture gallery contains many works of art, including certain examples from the French school. When Catherine II came to power, in line with her taste for classicism she chose to give a more austere aspect to this magnificent complex of buildings. To this end she had the gilded statues removed from the balustrade and the gildings of the façade painted over with a bronze colour. The annex in the Pompeian style, which with its completely incompatible character unhappily destroyed the unity of the whole, was also added at the time of Catherine II.

Rastrelli also deserves the credit for the Smolny Monastery project. In the museum of the Academy of Human Sciences at Leningrad, there

The Cathedral of St. Isaac, Leningrad, was altered many times before achieving its current form.

The Tauride Palace (1783–1789), given by Catherine II to her favourite, Potemkin, as a reward for his victory in the Crimea.

exists a model which demonstrates his original intentions: regrettably these have lost a great deal of their magnificence on account of the constant modifications made in the course of construction. This itself was a long-drawn-out process, and certain elements of the design were even abandoned as construction proceeded, e.g. the belfry. It is situated on the steep banks of the Neva, in the very place where the resin used in shipbuilding was produced under Peter the Great (*smola* means resin). Like all Rastrelli's works, Smolny was built in the Russian rococo style (the church and the other buildings date from 1748–1757). But the most striking feature is the harmonious blend of western influences with Russian tradition, making its first reappearance in this form in St. Petersburg. Rastrelli drew his inspiration for the church from the model provided by the Jesuit church, but also made use of elements drawn from Russian architectural tradition, i.e. the cross-shaped ground plan and the five gilded cupolas. The overall result was so convincing that Quarenghi, one of the architects of the classical style under Catherine II, never neglected to do him the honour, on passing by the Smolny Church, of doffing his hat with the words "That is what I call a church!" Nevertheless, on the artistic level Quarenghi's ideas were far removed from those of Rastrelli! The turquoise-blue walls with their ornamentation picked out in white impart a feeling of joyful freshness to this monastery, to which Elizabeth intended to retire in her old age.

The mark which Catherine II left on the architecture of St. Petersburg was in complete contrast to the lively style adopted by Elizabeth and her architects. Her sterner and more ascetic taste created a favourable climate for the inauguration of the classical period in Russia. This gave to St. Petersburg its majestic monumental aspect—its "austere beauty", sung by Pushkin—and in one form or another was pre-eminent in Russia for nearly a hundred years. This new direction in Russian art can be seen in a very large number of buildings: an example is the Maritime Exchange, constructed in the years from 1756 to 1813 at the extreme end of Basil Island by the architect Thomas de Thonon. The model for this edifice was the Temple of Poseidon at Paestum. It stands in stern beauty above the Neva, and is remarkable for the row of Doric columns which adorns the entire circumference of the building. On either side stands a 30-metre (100-foot) column serving as a lighthouse. Even more characteristic of this period is the Alexander Palace, built between 1792 and 1796 by Quarenghi, not far from Rastrelli's palace at Tsarskoe Selo. This palace, of which Catherine II made a gift to her grandson Alexander I, is one of the most imposing constructions of the 18th century. The eye is drawn to a colonnade which seems to open the palace on to the park. An impression of beauty and majestic grandeur emanates from the purity of its lines and the harmony of its proportions, which are not interrupted by any decorative devices on the walls.

The classical style also guided the construction of the palaces which Catherine had constructed for certain of her many favourites. The most generously treated were Potemkin and Gregory Orlov, who received from the hands of their sovereign and lover the Tauride Palace and the Marble Palace respectively. The latter was built for Orlov during the years 1768–1785 by Rinaldi, who balanced the austere simplicity of the forms with a covering of Siberian marble for the two upper storeys, the lower storey being of pink and grey granite. There are white pilasters placed between the granite panels, which give the palace a luxurious appearance in spite of the sobriety of the forms. The Tauride Palace was Potemkin's reward for the victory he had won in the Crimea.

The Cathedral of Our Lady of Kazan and the Cathedral St. Isaac, despite showing little originality of conception, nevertheless impose their monumental outlines on the profile of St. Petersburg. The construction of the former took ten years (1801–1811), the project and its execution being entrusted to the architect Voronikhin, who took as his model St. Peter's Square in Rome. The cathedral itself is surmounted by a cupola and forms the central element of the group; yet it appears almost slight in comparison with the colossal semicircular colonnade around it. Inside the cathedral the columns also have an important part to play, forming two rows which support a ceiling of sunken panels. The Cathedral of St. Isaac, which in its general appearance recalls the Pantheon in Paris, only arrived at its final form after a considerable number of revisions. Work was begun in 1768 under Rinaldi, on a spot where there already stood an earlier cathedral of the same name. The cathedral was to have five cupolas in accordance with Russian tradition; however, the work was never finished. Eventually it was demolished to make way for the present cathedral, which was finished in 1858 under Alexander II. Its unique and stately cupola rises to a height of 102 metres (335 feet) above sea-level.

But it would be unjust to evoke the beauty of St. Petersburg as it developed during the reigns of tsars whose tastes varied so widely, without mentioning one of its most important physical features—an element which both divides and unites the different parts of the town, which permits it to contemplate its own beauty as in a mirror, which caused Peter the Great's capital to be given the title of the "Venice of the North", and which, on a fine night, reflects back the clarity of the sky: in other words, the waters of the Neva, the Fontanka and the Moika. It is thanks to these that St. Petersburg, the Leningrad of the future, became and still remains unique in the world.

Expansion and Return to Sources

"The Marriage Proposal", by Fedotov.

The 19th century, in the course of which five tsars occupied the throne of Russia (Alexander I, Nicholas I, Alexander II, Alexander III and Nicholas II), is characterized in a historical context by the diversification of intellectual currents and artistic expression. The uncritical importation of western thought and art had been the rule during the previous century; now this was replaced by a nationalist movement, especially after the patriotic war against Napoleon in 1812. The rift which had opened up between the aristocracy and the people during the period when the door was open to the west was now partially bridged. This unity was very short-lived, however. The autocratic regime, harassed by demands from all sides—there were more than 700 peasant uprisings in this century—had periods of reforms alternating with periods of repression. The reforms concerned the institutions of the country and also its social organization: there was administrative reform in the setting up of local councils (zemstva) intended to play an important role in the economic and political life of the country, judicial reform with the creation of a new system of tribunals, military reform, and, above all, the abolition of serfdom in 1861. However, reforms suddenly ceased whenever the traditional structures of autocratic power were themselves in danger of being toppled. Death or deportation to Siberia were the

Right:
"The Temptation of Christ", by Kramskoi.

punishments that awaited rebels, whether their activity was political (the Decembrists) or artistic (Dostoievski).

The principal factor guiding the intellectual and artistic life of the 19th century was the re-establishment of Russian identity as a platform for the development of the country. This was aided by the growing number of Russians teaching in both ancient and new universities, by the work of scientists who were world-famous (e.g. Mendeleev and Pavlov) and, above all, by the creative activity of Russian writers, painters, musicians, sculptors and architects. They all helped to secure the replacement of the foreign artists who had been all-powerful during the previous century; and for them the evolution of Russia constituted the nucleus around which their concerns and their contemplations revolved. In some circles (the so-called Slavophiles) they went so far as to abjure the benefits of any sort of foreign input, proclaiming Russia as the creator of a new and more perfect civilization based on the ancient Russian moral, intellectual and spiritual values. The occidentalists opposed this view: for them the liberal or socialist theories from the west were an inspiration to the development of Russia. The ensuing debates were passionate, and found one outlet in the bias of the numerous scientific and literary reviews that sprang up in the 19th century, around which the more cultivated and enlightened minds in Russia polarized. The rediscovery

"Ivan the Terrible with the Corpse of his Son", by Repin

of traditional Russian values ran a course parallel to the quest for new motivating forces which would be capable of sustaining the development of the country. For in the 19th century Russia remained a prisoner of the outdated political and social structures, and for this reason failed to make up the two or three centuries by which it was lagging behind the countries of the west. This is the background against which the artistic life of Russia was to evolve, exposing great riches, during the 19th century.

When the 19th century dawned, Russian painting was still dominated by the themes and the techniques borrowed from the west. The evocation of national subjects remained the bread-and-butter work of the *liubki* and of painting in general, which was rather limited in scope. The subjects of the *liubki* could be religious, or drawn from the life of the tsar or from folk tales, or satirical (Napoleon being a favourite target at the beginning of the century). Genre-painting is represented essentially by three artists. Orlovski (1777–1832) illustrated different aspects of Russian life from about 1800–1830: men in the street, soldiers, and so on. Alexis Venetsianov preferred to rely on peasant life, depicting certain scenes with great authenticity, e.g. "The Barn", or "The Landowner Doing his Accounts". Fedotov, who like Venetsianov was self-taught, scrutinized the life and customs of the bourgeoisie, and recorded this in pictures such as "The New Rider" and "The Marriage Proposal". More than for the quality of their art these painters are interesting because they counterbalance the all-powerful Academy of Fine Arts at St. Petersburg, which ruled like a despot over the arts, and because they provide us with the first signs of realism in painting.

The painters turned out by the Academy at St. Petersburg found themselves compelled to ply their art on the lines imposed there, which they did until the year 1863, when a group of 13 students refused to treat the subject they were given and left the Academy to form the "Society for Travelling Exhibitions" under the direction of Ivan Kramskoi (1837–1887). The objectives of the association were twofold: to decentralize art, which at the time was limited to St. Petersburg, by travelling and presenting their work also in the provinces (hence the term "travelling exhibitions"); also to become involved in the social reality of the country, by using painting to denounce misery and injustice wherever

"The Boyarin Morozova", by Surikov.

they found it. If the society had a fault, it lay in their desire to make artistic expression secondary to subject matter. By neglecting artistic form they often prejudiced the quality of their works. Nevertheless, the fact remains that an entire series of distinguished painters emerged at this time in very different subject areas. Religious painting is represented above all by Ivan Kramskoi, who, having produced a series of portraits of great contemporary Russian writers (including Tolstoi, Nekrassov and Goncharov), attempted to give to the face of Christ features more closely representing Russian sensibility; see his painting "The Temptation of Christ". Vasnetsov produced the frescoes for the Church of St. Vladimir in Kiev, while Nestarov worked principally in Russian convents. Vassili Perov, after staying in Paris during 1863, specialized in genre-painting, which he enriched with numerous pictures of subjects drawn from everyday life. Examples are "The Arrival of the Governess", "The Easter Procession" and "The Discovery of the Icon", the satirical character of which is not concealed. Historical painting is best represented by Repin and Surikov, the first of whom is known principally for "The Volga Boatmen" (1870), symbolizing the oppression of the Russian people, and the pictures entitled "Ivan the Terrible with the Corpse of his Son" and "The Zaporozh Cossacks". Vassili Surikov recalls in his pictures the execution of the Streltsy, the fate of "The Boyarin Morozova", who refused to forswear her faith, and finally "The Conquest of Siberia". For the first time in the history of Russian painting, the Russian landscape took its place among the subjects treated. Kuinzhi specialized in painting the steppes of the Ukraine, but

Left to right:
Pushkin by Kiprenski; Mussorgski by Repin; Dostoievski by Perov.

Following pages:
"Eternal Rest", 1894. Levitan expresses in his work all the melancholy of the Russian landscape (Tretiakov Gallery, Moscow).

became famous for his "Birch Wood". The favourite subject of the Armenian painter Aivazovski was the sea, which, with its waves foaming under a cloudy sky, appears in more than 4,000 pictures. He also produced for Nicholas I a series of pictures showing the Russian ports.

However, art for art's sake had been neglected for so long that it inevitably became the main preoccupation of a new movement which grew up less than thirty years after the formation of the Society for Travelling Exhibitions. Its mouthpiece was the review *Mir Iskusstva*, which was directed by Alexandre Benois and Serge Diaghilev. Those artists and writers who allied themselves with the movement preached both the restoration of art to its former position, and more profound exchanges with foreign countries; in fact they felt particularly drawn to the works of the impressionists. The works of Vrubel (1856–1910) are fascinating, his tortured genius being close to madness. He painted watercolours in fine and harmonious colours, restored the frescoes of the Church of St. Cyril in Kiev, and went on to illustrate Lermontov's *The Demon*, for which he became famous. Isaac Levitan (1860–1900) expressed the melancholy of Russian landscapes; in his pictures celebrating nature in Russia this seems to reflect his own sadness. There are different portrayals of autumn and of twilight, and of the steppes and rivers, the unending sweep of which is interrupted only by the cupolas of some monastery. The portrait also has its place in the new movement, thanks to the brush of Valentin Serov (1865–1911), which was greatly appreciated by the tsar Nicholas II and the court personnages—the princesses Yussupov and Orlov—whose portraits he painted. There were also painters of this period who were attracted by the theatre, e.g. Golovin, Benois and Bakst. They created sets that perfectly complemented the music and the dance. This Russian concept of theatre reached its ultimate fulfilment in the creation of the Ballet Snegurochka in 1880 and achieved popularity in the west at the start of the 20th century through the *Ballets Russes* of Diaghilev (e.g. *Sheherazade, Prince Igor, The Firebird*).

The 19th century is, however, above all the great century of Russian literature and music. Incomparable literary masterpieces were produced which today are known the world over. Russian writers defied the censure which greeted any work bearing the stamp of freedom or criticizing social misery and political terror; they braved the perils of exile in some

Above and left:
The madrasa of Abdul Azizghan. Central Asia had enjoyed a glorious economic and cultural past, and a flourishing civilization. This wealth was reflected in the construction of numerous mosques and madrasas and of strikingly beautiful towns.

Opposite page, top:
The Kahyan tower, a minaret dating from 1127.

Opposite page, bottom:
The gates of the ancient town of Bukhara.

Below:
Samarkand. Top to bottom: Registan Square; Chak-i-Zihba; Tamerlane's tomb.

remote province or garrison. Songs in verse and in prose were penned in honour of Russia, expressing in lines of rare beauty the love that the Russian writers felt for their people, however fierce their criticism of them.

The beginning of the 19th century witnessed the childhood and growth of the first and greatest Russian poet—Pushkin (1799–1837). His lines have a beauty that does not survive translation, and play on the Russian language as on a musical instrument; they leave all those who yearn for love and freedom profoundly moved. But although the sentiments he expressed are universal, his work remains deeply rooted in Russian soil, and it is only there that it can be fully comprehended. Best known for his poems—*Russlan and Ludmilla, Eugene Onegin, Poltava, Boris Godunov*—which in turn were an inspiration to Russian composers and dramatists, he also wrote a number of prose works, such as *Queen of Spades* and *The Captain's Daughter*. Pushkin was succeeded by Lermontov, an altogether more romantic and religious poet who wrote *Death of the Poet* in his honour. All his lyrical energy is employed in poems such as *The Angel* and, above all, *The Demon* (a subject borrowed by the painter Vrubel) for which his inspiration was the beauty of the Caucasus. He also wrote the beautiful poem *Borodino* and the novel *A Hero of our Time* before being killed in a duel—the fate which had also befallen Pushkin. Gogol (1802–1852) was one of the first of the great novelists of the 19th century. His works are characterized by satire and realism, and paint a picture of provincial Russian society, for example in *The Inspector-general* and *Dead Souls*. Later he turned to fantasy in the short stories *The Nose* and *The Overcoat*. But it was above all during the second half of the 19th century that Russian writers enriched world literature with their immortal works. Among them was Dostoievski (1821–1881), whose involvement with a clandestine group drawing its inspiration from the theories of Proudhon, Fourier and Saint-Simon was rewarded with penal servitude in Siberia. He emerged more mature from this experience, which is described in *The House of the Dead*, and wrote works in which the spiritual dimension is fully treated—*Crime and Punishment* among them. But Dostoievski's great strength lay in his ability to plumb the depths of human psychology and to have grasped man's unconscious in all its complexity. It is by his handling of psychology that he succeeds in depicting human suffering. *The Idiot* is especially remarkable, as is *The Brothers Karamazov*, which remains his most demanding and most con-

troversial novel. The work of Turgenev (1818–1883) is of an entirely different type. He stayed on the fringes of the various conservative and revolutionary movements, and eventually a degree of isolation prompted him to emigrate to France. In his works he depicts more than anything else a Russia doomed soon to disappear: *Fathers and Sons, Virgin Soil* and his poems in prose.

In 1828 the giant among Russian writers was born—the man whom Turgenev described to Yasnaia Poliana as "*the* great writer of Russia": Leon Tolstoi. His output falls into two phases. The first includes his autobiographical accounts *Childhood, Boyhood* and *Youth*, and *Anna*

Bottom:
Echmiadzin, in Armenia, the foundations of which date from the 5th century, is still the spiritual capital of the Armenians.

Arakelots Church (874) is characteristic of original Armenian architecture, which influenced among others the architecture of Suzdalia.

Karenina and *War and Peace*, in which he describes persons who are full of life, so authentic that they are very close to us in their sentiments, passions and ideals. In the second phase of his creative activity, Tolstoi turned his back on life, with its joy and its suffering: he even went so far as to renounce his earlier works so as to devote himself exclusively to religion, which in his view should be stripped of all mysticism so as to become the foundation for a new conception of the world, for a new life. He preached his faith, the necessity for a simple life and the renunciation of wealth, in *Confession, In this I believe* and *The Kingdom of the Gods is in us*. In these works his language is perfectly clear and accessible to everybody, so that his concepts of God and of justice were conveyed to the hearts of a great number of his fellow men. Towards the end of his life he returned to a more literary and less prophetic style in *Resurrection* and *Kreutzer Sonata*.

From the end of the 19th and beginning of the 20th centuries we have the writings of two very different authors—Chekhov and Gorki. By contrast with the majority of authors, Chekhov had little to do with the political debate. He was more interested in the meanness and shabbiness of the middle classes and their customs, describing and denouncing them in an often delightful fashion. He became famous above all as a playwright, notably for four plays: *The Seagull, Uncle Vanya, Three Sisters* and *The Cherry Orchard*. The path of Gorki (1868–1936) was altogether different: isolated from the majority of writers mentioned so far by his

origins and his life, he very quickly found himself closely involved in revolutionary circles. He preferred active heroes and faith in the future to the disaffected intellectuals and the pessimism of Chekhov. At first his works bear the stamp of a sort of revolutionary romanticism (e.g. *Foma Gordeyev, Lower Depths, Childhood* and *My Universities*), but they later acquire a more incisive and demanding character.

The authors mentioned here are those who are best known outside the frontiers of Russia, but there are many other writers, such as Alexander Herzen, Nekrassov and Saltikov-Shchedrin to name but three, whose works contributed towards channelling the main streams of Russian thought in the 19th century. Above all they sought the truth in their descriptions of a country and a people whom in many ways they helped to rediscover their identity.

Georgian gold: triptych from Khakhuli, 10th–12th century. This is an important piece of decorative art from medieval Georgia.

But in cultural terms the various regions which came under the political control of St. Petersburg had little, very little, in common. Russia had in fact launched itself very quickly into the conquest of lands which had their own cultural and religious traditions, and these were quite distinct from those of the Russians, as well as being more ancient. In the 17th century Ivan the Terrible conquered the khanates of Kazan and Astrakhan and imposed his rule on these two Moslem states. The Crimean Tartars and Siberia were overcome in the 18th century. Russian expansion into Central Asia began in Kazakhstan, which was inhabited mainly by nomads, and ended in 1884 in Turkestan, of which the three principalities (the emirate of Bukhara and the khanates of Kokand and Khiva) had seen exceptional cultural advancement. The inhabitants had long since been converted to Islam and settled down to live principally in the fertile regions and in towns such as Bukhara and

Samarkand, with their illustrious past. Trade was flourishing, and the building of the magnificent mosques was an outward sign of this prosperity. The blue cupolas and the minarets served once as beacons to guide the caravans wending their way, laden with precious merchandise, from east to west; and now they still surmount fabulous towns that seem to come straight from the *Thousand and One Nights*. But this region fell victim to tribal strife, which paved the way for the advance of the Russians and for their eventual supremacy in the area.

Georgia possessed a cultural tradition that was already several thousand years old when that country was annexed to Russia in 1801. It had benefited by its exceptionally favourable situation, enriched from the earliest times by contact with Greece, the Scythians and the Near East and influenced by the adoption of christianity as official state religion

during the 4th and 5th centuries. In the 10th century Georgia ruled over the whole of the Caucasus. There are numerous places such as Vardzia, city of rock, and Mtskheta, the ancient royal capital of Iberia, and numerous churches and works of art—notably gold and silver ware—which bear witness to this splendid past. The presence of the Russians in the Caucasus was consolidated with the annexation of eastern Armenia in 1826–1828, although a large part of the country remained under the bloodthirsty domination of the Turks, who had siezed it in 1064. It was during the two centuries prior to this that Armenian art and culture enjoyed their golden age. However, vestiges of Armenian art and architecture from as far back as the 5th century are known; the most notable feature is the construction of churches that are original in form, and which, in their conception, influenced Russian architecture in general and that of Suzdalia in particular.

Above left:
Reliquary: cloisonné enamel, 12th century.

Above:
The Crucifixion: 16th-century Georgian icon in gold, silver, rubies, turquoises and pearls.